THE SCIENTIFIC FALLACY
AND POLITICAL MISUSE
OF THE CONCEPT OF RACE

THE SCIENTIFIC FALLACY
AND POLITICAL MISUSE
OF THE CONCEPT OF RACE

Ronald E. Hall

Symposium Series
Volume 79

The Edwin Mellen Press
Lewiston•Queenston•Lampeter

Library of Congress Cataloging-in-Publication Data

Hall, Ronald E.
  The scientific fallacy and political misuse of the concept of race / Ronald E. Hall.
    p. cm. -- (Symposium series ; v. 79)
  Includes bibliographical references and index.
  ISBN 0-7734-6372-0
    1. Racism--United States--History. 2. Race--Political aspects--United States--History. 3. Race--Philosophy. 4. African Americans--Social conditions. 5. African Americans--Civil rights--History. 6. United States--Race relations. 7. Slavery--United States--History. 8. Slavery--America--History. I. Title. II. Symposium series (Edwin Mellen Press) ; v. 79.

E184.A1H2135 2004
320.5'6'0973--dc22

                                                          2004051961

This is volume 79 in the continuing series
Symposium Series
Volume 79 ISBN 0-7734-6372-0
SS Series ISBN 0-88946-989-X

A CIP catalog record for this book is available from the British Library

The Edwin Mellen Press   The Edwin Mellen Press
Box 450   Box 67
Lewiston, New York   Queenston, Ontario
USA 14092-0450   CANADA L0S 1L0

The Edwin Mellen Press, Ltd.
Lampeter, Ceredigion, Wales
UNITED KINGDOM SA48 8LT

Printed in the United States of America

Dedicated to Marsha, Karen, and Crystal for what might have been.

No white American, including those who insist that opportunities exist for persons of every race, would change places with even the most successful black American.

Andrew Hacker, 1992

Table of Contents

	Preface	i
	Foreword by Dr. George T. Rowan	1
I	Introduction	3
II	The Atlantic Slave Trade	19
III	Race	37
IV	Quadroons, Octoroons, and Mulattoes	51
V	Fear/Inferiority: Racist Images of African-American Men	65
VI	Affirmative Action: The Racial Divide	79
VII	The Politics of Race	93
VIII	Racism in the 21st Century	107
IX	From Race to Reason	127
	References	141
	Index	159

Preface

We have just recently crossed the threshold of a new millennium and find ourselves no less threatened by the woes of race than in years past. Long before Euro-American scholars were willing to admit, the world renowned African-American scholar W.E.B. DuBois, in *Souls of Black Folk* proclaimed the problem of the 20th century as the "problem of the color-line." Race then as today was frequently noted by skin color. That being so, we find ourselves grappling with an issue long past the time it should have been resolved.

Some would argue that race is American and without the concept of race our sovereignty would be forced to completely redefine itself. We have relied on race in the conduct of our daily lives, the direction of our institutions, and overall as a quality of life harbinger. Thus, Americans of different races are obviously similar in genetic structure: both frequent a common existential space and both rely on nourishment from the environment of that space to evolve. However, akin to the contrived significance of race our environmental evolution within that space may differ dramatically. Those of us, such as African-Americans stained by the rumors of inferiority, are then burdened by the prescripts of race that amount to a constant drain on our humanity. In human genes, as in the quality of life, Americans may have much in common, but they encounter distinct American experiences due to race.

Perhaps the ability of race to have prevailed for such an extended period of time and become so endemic to the American experience is associated with its utility. Despite the concept of race as a proven biological fallacy its legitimacy is sustained without question. Its potency is perpetuated by the social, political, and economic vehicles of society merely for purposes of oppression. Hence, because race is a fallacy those who engage in oppression on the basis of race do so purely by means of rhetoric because race cannot be objectively quantified in the scientific sense. In the aftermath both victim and the perpetrator of race are demarcated by its prevalence. Those who abhor oppression on the basis of race and labor for its elimination have failed by their inability to provide an accurate analysis of the problem. What is more, the victims of oppression have been no less given to the norms and value systems of those who would oppress as a matter of socio-political and cultural consequence. Subsequently, the DuBoisian reference to skin color (race) as a 20th century problem will carry on into the 21st century without a critical dissection of its being.

Recently, there has been considerable attention given to affirmative action litigation for the supposed unraveling of race. These cases attest to the willingness of those who are normally the guardians of race to oppress in the absence of race, but oppress via race nonetheless. Just beneath the surface of their acts is the reinforcement of a concept fashioned to suit the new millennium. This form of oppression could characterize race in the new era. In calls for diversity and minority group conservatism it will cross lines of ethnicity, class, gender, and other group demarcations. Such oppression is then multi-group in every sense that will require a universally collective effort to resolve. Once the victims of oppression understand this fundamental issue, and are willing to take a leadership role and engage the perpetrators of oppression the race oppression of the 20th century will be eliminated. The intensity of this effort will correlate in proportion to 1) the ability of Euro-, African-, Asian-, and Native-Americans to gauge the phenomenon; and 2) the miscegenation of individual and group norms that will provide a willingness to prioritize counter-race-based behaviors. Thus, in the 21st century we will face enormous challenges and perhaps much anguish. Conversely, it will also be a time of profound change. The most profound of these changes will be the analysis of race that will enable the comprehension of oppression as what it is: a national, global and universal phenomenon that functions to stabilize and assure the current world order. Our willingness to confront this evil will move us from race to reason.

Ronald E. Hall, Ph.D.
Michigan State University
2003

Foreword

Although it is a distant era in history, Americans in particular continue to manifest the impact of slavery and colonization. This is most prevalent among African Americans especially African American males in the area of health. For instance if you are fifteen years old and a white female in the State of Michigan you have a ninety-two percent chance of living to age sixty-five. If you are a fifteen-year old black male in Michigan you have less than a sixty-percent chance of living to age sixty-five. Among Americans, there remain citizens who are committed to the best interests of their fellow man while hardly acknowledging any reference at all to the implications of racism. Politicians dominated by ideology have failed the nation. Furthermore, those who teach at some of our most prestigious universities, that serve a substantial minority population, haven't the faintest idea of how the implications of race have limited the nation's potential.

As one who values knowledge, I have agonized over the manner in which race given American influence has been regarded worldwide. On more than one occasion, I have encountered students and professors, who are trained to handle the keenest aspects of emotional and psychological adjustment with hardly any consideration given to the social and cultural gaps perpetuated by decades of oppression and racial discrimination because in a post-60s era such issues have become passe. For many reasons, racism in practically every sector of the academy and the society at-large has remained an unspeakable taboo. This, I see as dangerous. It serves the tenets of racists and their colonial status quo. In the aftermath African-American and other so-called minority groups are impeded by race.

Some of my colleagues in academia will argue that to write about the unspeakable and passé issue of race will do more harm than good because it is so provocative. But it is my opinion that confronting such a provocative topic literally is a healthy and socially appropriate way to benefit Americans of all races and ultimately humanity in general. In essence, a rising tide lifts all boats and although it can only be a start, a start is where solutions begin.

In conclusion, I believe the problem for any writer who attempts to characterize a group of which he is not a member will always be that he may ultimately make errors of interpretation, which a native would not. When that interpretation reaches publication, we run the risk of doing disservice to all. In the grist of self worth, I have determined dignity and respect for all people, regardless of race should take precedent. The solution for me lies in maintaining openness and a willingness to confront new ideas. Furthermore, those of us impeded by the mistruths of racism and the inferiority associated with our race indulge an extremely dangerous luxury. By virtue of victimization in modern circles of scholarship there is a tendency to portray us as simultaneously the embodiment of quintessential virtue and cultural piety. Our denigration by Western civilization has cast upon us an unchangeable cloak of integrity and innate nobility setting us morally apart from our oppressors. We seem to feel that because we are most often the victims of racism, that we have done all we could to enable its elimination. We take no responsibility for lack of action and have deluded ourselves into ignoring the devastation because America is such a wealthy nation. However in the final analysis, humanity, of whatever race, ethnicity, gender, or class cannot deny the dignity and worth of another without diminishing some measure of its own. For in the image of one's victim, is a reflection of one's self. Believing that, it is my sincerest hope that those who read this book are enabled to move from race to reason in cooperation with their fellow man.

George T. Rowan, Ph.D.
Professor, Resource Development
Michigan State University

I

Introduction

Americans and other Western scientists refer to race as a biological differentiation of humanity on the basis of genetic criteria. In this context race may be harmless and indeed a contribution to science. In the evolution of knowledge, differentiation is necessary to enable science hence human quality of life. Science applies differentiation to flora to produce the best quality of plants. Scientists even differentiate for the purposes of healthy fauna to ensure viable offspring. Such manifestations of differentiation are ethically sound and germane to civilization. Differentiation by race as applied to humanity has not been so benign. It is unethical and enables the unfair practices extended from Western civilization in its enslavement of Negroid race people. In the West, race differentiation is a prelude to inferiority and the oppression of those among non-Caucasoid races. The most visible impact is manifested in current day America.

As every U.S. citizen who is the least bit knowledgeable about American history knows, this country is a legacy of immigration.[1] Immigrants of any number and combination of so-called racial categories left their native lands under various circumstances in pursuit of the "American Dream." On arrival, those of European descent who were designated as members of the Caucasian race and those who looked Caucasian experienced a substantially different America than their Negroid and Mongoloid race counterparts. All but members of Caucasian race groups were characterized as inferior and otherwise unfit to be structurally assimilated into the mainstream of society.[2] Their racial heritage was rationalized as a handicap, which prevented them from contributing as productive members of an advanced technological culture. Thus, despite evidence to the contrary, non-Europeans remain peripheral to the mainstream, having their skills, talents, loyalty and pursuit of the "American Dream" compromised by race.

Race as the crux of Western civilization is a function of the racial status quo. African inferiority, extended from the Atlantic slave trade necessitated the Caucasoid European perception of Negroid people as genetically fitted for bondage. Thus, the end of slavery and Western colonization in Africa, Asia, and the Americas did not permit Africans to sit as equals amidst their European counterparts. African-Americans—representative of Negroid peoples the world over—have not been accorded the respect as ordinary human beings. They remain similarly oppressed by race in housing, law, politics, and other facets of American life. Consequently, the issue of race—associated with European aggression—has become central in the lives of Euro- and African-Americans in the struggle to end the various forms of race-based practices.

As a function of Western civilization, race in America has been consistently portrayed on the basis of inferiority as if racial identity were the demarcation of different species of man. In the aftermath is a belief that the only significant elements of humanity are members of Caucasian race groups. Negroid and Mongoloid race groups have been less capable of the milestones of civilization. In fact, inferiority in America and elsewhere extends beyond the various categories of race, including those criteria similar to and associated with Negroid races. Seldom discussed is inferiority on the basis of race, extending from brutalities directed at post-enslaved peoples. As a legacy of slavery, the history of race can be witnessed by any visitor to the Americas. However, because race has been couched in science, racists have been inclined to apply it in the effect of oppressive policy.

No doubt, the single issue of race does not exist independent of other factors that contribute to oppression. Furthermore, the myth of "white supremacy" for the most part is no longer fashionable in society or academia. Such a myth though shattered in the scholarly literature and banished from the circles of polite society, remains largely intact on the basis of science. The scientific conclusions are most apparent in the actuality of everyday life among the great masses of diverse people in America. Regarding those of African, Asian, Latino, and Native descent, race has become the mark of inferiority. Race figures—however tacitly—in their daily oppression and will clearly continue to do so until the residue of slavery is completely dissipated.

Race is the most fundamental and defining issue in America and Western civilization. Despite rhetoric to the contrary and that posits a color-blind society is the ultimate ideal, in America race is the determining factor for quality of life vis-à-vis groups and individuals. The evidence is inherent in the extent of race consciousness, which Americans exhibit in their norms, values, institutions, and social space. For example, segregation in housing, churches, and friendships until recently was accepted as norm in an effort to prevent non-Euro-Americans from aspiring and reaching the American Dream. By means of race they were destined to the most trite of circumstances and penalized if attempted to do otherwise.

Fortunately, the aforementioned was not the path to which non-Europeans ascribed. African-, Latino-, Asian-, and Native-American groups have waged a constant struggle in an effort to take their place as equals within society. It would be a mistake to dismiss this analysis of the American race issue as without Euro-American support, too "pessimistic," or perhaps "antiquated" and/or "impossible." Even so, much of the Euro-American mainstream remains convinced that the antebellum assumptions about race, extended from the Atlantic slave trade are based on scientific fact.[3] Few 21st century scholars have dared invest their livelihood and professional reputations in challenging this misperception. Aside from such risks are ultimately concerns for the betterment of this democracy. America must find a way to confront what it has so long ignored in the validation of race. It must be open and willing to accept responsibility for its human oppression if for no other reason than to do so opens a window to the past and provides a benchmark to measure how far it has come and has to go in the yet foreseeable future.

Sustaining ignorance pertaining to so-called race is the fact that, while it is a Eurocentric concept, Euro-Americans, i.e., Caucasians remain uncomfortable in public discussions about race. Race is a complex and deeply divisive issue they would rather avoid at all costs, even though it is endemic and deeply woven into the fabric of American life. Ironically Euro-American scientists, philosophers, educators, and others continue to make race-based assumptions about the various groups in ordering society.[4] The same Americans who discourage race discussions in polite conversations regard it as a fundamental issue in discussions about poverty, education, crime, music, sports, sex, intelligence, etc. They ignore "radical" anthropologists, biologists, and geneticists who question the biological (in)significance of "race." As a result, society is further confused by pseudo-science and the contradiction it prolongs. Ultimately, more questions about the validity of race complicate an already complex issue, which carries it further from the minds of polite conversationalists for fear they will be perceived as ignorant or, at worst, as racists.

In order for Americans to move beyond the impediments of race they must comprehend the development and evolution of the American experience. Included are an understanding of its origins and characteristic features, the political culture, and how it evolved to its present day status. No doubt, the common racial views embraced by Americans during the antebellum differ to some extent from those held by most Americans today.[5] However that difference should not presume that a more liberal and enlightened perspective will prevail, either into the long term or immediate future. Conflicts might very well amplify, particularly in an era of increasing racial diversity brought about by more tolerant immigration policies and a reduction in the proportion of Euro-Americans.[6] If not attended to, the consequences will threaten the sanctity of this democracy in its ability to survive as a preferred manifestation of diversity and as an unprecedented experiment in nation building.

The call for more racial diversity came about only recently. Social activists in the 1960s prompted Congress to amend immigration policies so as to eliminate "racist" quotas that made it all but impossible for immigrants to arrive from other than nations in Europe.[7] Associated with supplementary historical events, as well as differential fertility rates among the races, America is presenting a much different account of racial composition. During the 1960s, when such changes were being advocated, the U.S. was 88.6% Euro-American, 10.5% African-American, and less than 1% Asian- or other-American. Today, Euro-Americans comprise less than 74% of the total population, while African-, Latino-, and Asian-Americans account for 13%, 9%, and 4% respectively.[8] What is more at present better than 830,000 immigrants enter the U.S. legally while better than 300,000 enter the country illegally. All but a few are from "Third World" or non-European nations. These numbers exceed those who migrate in the rest of the world combined.[9] That being so, the U.S. Bureau of Census has determined that the proportion of Euro-Americans will decrease to 64% by 2020 and less than 50% by the year 2050. However, such estimates are likely understated given that so-called Negroid and Mongoloid race groups are migrating to the U.S. in greater numbers than census calculations can accommodate. For this reason and others, America must come to terms with its race issue.

If calculations of the U.S. Bureau of Census are correct and if Third World races continue to migrate to America in greater numbers than Caucasians from Europe, America will witness an unprecedented event in population statistics. That event will likely account for the conversion of a once dominant, Euro-American population into a racial minority at some point. Consequently the U.S. will have evolved into undoubtedly the most racially diverse nation the world has yet known.[10] To some these facts illustrate a disturbing trend. Euro-American social scientists and the population at-large have given little thought to preparation for changes in both policy and society such a trend will bring. Current discussions about race remain antiquated and directed by Eurocentric conservative agendas (11). Hence, Myrdal's 1944 classic, *An American Dilemma*, is no less disturbing today than it was then.

Regarding the business of nation building, America is a social experiment that has not yet reached its full potential. Race is the tenacious impediment that accounts for its struggling pace. Suffice it to say that in more than a half century after Myrdal's revelation Euro-Americans remain fearful of other race groups. These fears hearken back to the 19th century antebellum era and Euro-American suspicions posed in the wake of both a sizeable slave population as well as a hostile Native-American population. Such suspicions have prevailed as a consequence of the race issue. What social scientists of that day did not realize is that, while African-Americans were the immediate victims of bondage, consequences were not irrelevant to slave masters. In the backdrop of slavery was a devastating denunciation of the emerging republic. That denunciation was an intractable denigration of its democratic ideals to the core thereby securing race to the American conscience.[12]

Although slavery and the antebellum era are bygone historical tragedies, African-Americans in particular continue to manifest the impact of bondage. Among social scientists, there remain professionals who are trained with hardly any reference at all to the far reaching implications of race as it pertains to quality of life. Academic journals of social work, psychology, sociology, etc., dominated by a Eurocentric perspective have failed accordingly to take notice. Furthermore, those who teach at some of America's most prestigious universities that serve a substantial African-American population, do not have the faintest idea of how the implications of race extended from slavery impact the social environment of African-Americans today. Being members of an inferior designated race directly correlates to their welfare and overall quality of life.

The employment status of Africa-Americans has had a clear impact on their quality of life.[13] That impact has contributed to the issues for which many seek social workers for help. Conversely, employment status among Euro-Americans, while not irrelevant, has a different impact and is arguably less disruptive to their quality of life. Euro-Americans who control quality of life resources have not acknowledged this fact injecting bias into statistics. To what extent does employment status differ for African- and Euro-Americans? What are the implications of that difference for quality of life and the perception of African-American, i.e., Negroid, races as inferior?

Any reference to African-American quality of life that does not consider employment is biased at best and racist at worst. The influence of Eurocentric perspectives has reinforced the perception of African-Americans as social and economic failures without acknowledging their historically prevalent, socio-economic circumstances. The ability of African-Americans to be employed is directly correlated in predicting their quality of life. This fact is substantiated by research that suggests that African-American fathers view their role essentially as that of provider.[14] Subsequently research further suggests that African-American fathers show a marked increase in the number of hours worked following the birth of their first child.[15] Unfortunately, according to the Department of Labor, the unemployment rate for African-American men in 1988 was 19.4% as compared to 7.4% for Euro-American men. What is more, even Euro-American women had lower rates of unemployment than African-American men at 6.7%.[16]

More recent unemployment rates for African-Americans have been no less discouraging. In 1992 and 1993, the unemployment rates for those between the ages of 20 and 24 were an astounding 24.5 and 23.0 percents. Unemployment rates for Euro-Americans of the same age during the same time period were 10.4 and 9.5 percent. For African-Americans over 25 years of age unemployment rates were 11.7 and 10.5 percent for the years 1992 and 1993. For their Euro-American counterpart unemployment rates were 5.8 and 5.2 percent during the same years.

The employment status of African-Americans is critical to the assessment and perceptions of racial inferiority. In times of both economic growth and economic turmoil the employment status of African-Americans has lagged behind that of Euro-Americans considerably. This fact is significant, despite sexual equality, the male is continually viewed as the principal provider of the American family's financial well-being. In addition, the literature suggests that such perceptions are even more indicative of African-American families.[17] In the aftermath, while African-Americans adhere to the more traditional view of fatherhood, they have minimal opportunity to fulfill such a role compared to Euro-Americans. That gap in opportunity is driven by employment status as pertains to economics but is assumed to be reflective of racial inferiority. This discrepancy between perception and reality is characteristic of race rhetoric and relevant to the difficulties sustained by African-Americans trying to maintain a quality of life commensurate with talent and hard work.[18]

As a matter of fact, race-based unemployment for African-Americans is a major factor in their inability to assimilate into the mainstream of society. This is most apparent in the direct correlation between the state of the economy and the viability of African-American life.[19] With few exceptions, it has been consistently demonstrated that commensurate with improvement in the economy vis-à-vis employment is the success of African-American quality of life. Current quality of life difficulties are thus attributable to the economy and not to racial inferiority, as racists would suggest.

In a patriarchal society such as America, employment is the keystone to achievement of the traditional fatherhood role. A man's inability to find work can have a devastating psychological impact. In reference to Mexican-Americans, Sotomayor contends that the subjection of men to low status and unemployment contributes to undermining their role as father, provider, disciplinarian, and protector, which have direct implications for not only quality of life but manhood as well.[20] In a culture where the concept of machismo is strong, this can be traumatic. In the aftermath are consequences for the family system including a disruption in the family's decision-making patterns, equilibrium, and, hence, inability to navigate a hostile environment. Thus, when assessing African-American quality-of-life efforts accuracy requires the differentiation between normal family structure and an attempt to adjust to a hostile socio-economic environment. For example, there is obvious differentiation between a father who is absent via lifestyle and one who is absent because he cannot fulfil the traditional role of father for lack of employment.

The racial implications of employment relative to African-American quality of life are further complicated by the employment status of women. In a culture where men are valued for what they earn, men who do not earn are seen as less eligible by African-American women.[21] Women in the U.S. traditionally marry upward socio-economically and men marry downward, further complicating the implications of employment.[22] What is more, among the various ethnic groups African-American women have historically been employed at higher rates than Euro-American women. For a myriad of reasons, African-American women have had fewer alternatives, which unfortunately does not negate the fact. No doubt the historical ability of the African-American community to sustain itself economically has been contingent on the employment of African-American women. Thus, the question racists have failed to ask about the inferiority of Negroid racial groups is: what are the consequences of the woman's employment status regarding the ability of their men to fulfil the fatherhood role? Regardless of race and/or ethnicity it would appear that the employment of women in a patriarchy, at the expense of men, would have overwhelming consequences for respect and quality of life. Moreover, the consequences of employing African-American women differs from those of employing Euro-American women. The most significant of difference is the fact that, even when both African-American men and women are employed, in any given situation women earn a higher percentage of the total family income than do their Euro-American counterparts. According to the National Commission on Working Women, African-American women earn 82 % of the incomes of their male counterparts.[23] The same statistic for Euro-American women in similarly situated families is 67 %. Earning differentials between African- and Euro-American women may suggest African-American women command greater family authority than do Euro-American women. Such disparity is exacerbated nationally. Furthermore, while a major element of the country struggles with dual employment issues many African-American families are struggling with the prospect of having at least one full-time principal earner. For men in particular, those who are employed may be "underemployed" to the extent they work seasonally or otherwise intermittently. Future scenarios also appear bleak as the high school dropout rate for African-American males continues to be higher than that for females.[24] In a capitalistic society where wealth translates into power, this can have an impact on perceptions of racial inferiority and quality of life.[25]

In the outcomes of employment status, African-American women have had a differential impact on the quality of life compared to that of Euro-American women. This would accommodate a more equitable distribution of decision-making, including that normally assumed by the patriarch.[26] Closely associated with the more equitable distribution of decision-making is a more positive assessment of African-American women by Euro-American researchers at the expense of African-American men and their assessment as competent, able citizens.[27] By no means does this suggest that African-American women are the key to race problems in their group. Both men and women exist within the same oppressive environment. However, the sex-role boundaries between African-American men and women have become less defined as a consequence of employment status. While not the essential variable, this cannot be assumed to be irrelevant.[28] Given the dynamics of sex-role boundaries it is possible that some among African-American men may feel threatened by women's increased authority and employment status. This situation contrasts with the Euro-American woman and her authority. As the employment status of African-American men remains inferior to that of women in a society where men are valued as earners such men may feel more psychological threats from their women than Euro-American men in similar circumstances. This suggestion is supported by research in that the earnings of African-American women, relative to their husbands, were found to be a significant source of tension.[29] Succinctly put, the marriages most at risk for divorce were those in which women earned more than 40 percent of the family income.[30]

More dramatic than the race-based economic correlations to African-American quality of life is what African-American males in particular have experienced. In a patriarchy, males of outgroup races are a constant threat to the mainstream. That threat necessitates their being singled out for various acts of brutality and other manifestations of their racial differentiation. However, it is those of Negroid groups, i.e., African-Americans, who have encountered the focus of brutality particularly from law enforcement despite their status as law abiding citizens. The most common occurrence takes place on American roads.

While motorists harassed by exuberant law enforcement officers are frequently disturbed by the effort to ensure traffic safety it is arguably the race of such motorists that enables their assumed culpability. Assumptions of culpability by law enforcement officers have sparked controversy and protest. In fact, assault of African-Americans by law enforcement officers frequently has little to do with traffic safety and is arguably attributable to their race particularly where males are concerned.[31] Race is the universal factor of those victimized for what is commonly ordinary behavior. The constant subjection of African-American motorists to biased traffic norms is racist and extends from the universal perception of Negroid races as inferior.

African-Americans remain constantly aware of their race in all matters of public affairs. Vilification has contributed to the victimization of such Americans as a racist stereotype who cannot conform to the racial norms of mainstream American society.[32] Hence, in comparison to Caucasians, African-Americans having darker skin are, more often than any other racial, ethnic, gender, social/culture group, falsely accused of being active participants in criminal activity.[33] And given the power of media to impose and to monitor norms, such victimization may keep African-Americans, who are otherwise ordinary law abiding citizens, under constant emotional and psychological stress.

On the New Jersey turnpike, a 42-year-old dentist has been pulled over by state troopers more than fifty times during his commuting to work. Dr. Elmo Randolph is not a careless driver. In fact, despite being frequently pulled over by police, Dr. Randolph has never been issued a ticket. Each time the state troopers stopped the dentist the questions were routine: "Do you have any drugs or weapons in your car?"[34] Dr. Randolph drives a gold BMW and, being an African-American male, obviously is not Caucasian. For years African-Americans like Dr. Randolph have complained about being humiliated by racist law enforcement policies without anything being done. The position of the police is that race is irrelevant to being stopped on the turnpike; but, in fact, skin color is the cue to race and being stopped, according to three African-Americans and one Hispanic-American who were shot by troopers.

As the four Americans drove along the turnpike in a rented van, police pulled them over and opened fire, striking three and critically wounding two of them. At police headquarters, officers contend the suspects were stopped because radar showed the van to be traveling at an excessive rate of speed. The department where the officers were stationed was forced to admit later that they had no radar equipment. The circumstances for the shooting are currently under investigation.

Aside from the shootings, the most troubling aspect of this New Jersey incident is the fact that no less than three years earlier a New Jersey judge concluded that troopers were practicing racial profiling. Instead of doing what was necessary to eradicate such racism from the ranks of law enforcement, the New Jersey Attorney General sided with the troopers to appeal the case. After the case reached public awareness, the Attorney General declined to pursue it because of his concern for winning a political office.

It would appear that racism reaches every level of the American judicial system regardless of Negroid groups, extending a constant source of stress that is otherwise irrelevant to Euro-American law abiding citizens. That the problem in New Jersey is so pervasive is exemplified by a decision of the United States Justice Department to intervene should the governor of that state decide to ignore racial incidents.

The constant stresses of racism experienced by African-Americans should come as no surprise because it permeates law enforcement policies. For example, the state of New Jersey eventually admitted that the State Police targeted certain motorists for drug searches along the New Jersey Turnpike.[35] These tactics, while racist and unethical, are common in Russia, where the KGB recruits members of the community to spy on its citizenry. In New Jersey, law enforcement has recruited motel workers to spy on patrons who speak Spanish—a language associated with Negroid and Mongoloid race groups. In New York, law enforcement denies the use of "racial profiling," but a recent story in *Crain's New York Business* raises serious questions.[36] The newspaper interviewed twenty professionals who all gave detailed accounts of their experiences with racial profiling, having been singled out and humiliated by police, usually for driving expensive cars.

This kind of ongoing racism has deepened feelings of alienation among affluent and law abiding African-American professionals who had hoped that success would allow them to become mainstream citizens. However, instead of fading into the American patchwork, they have become an ever more popular target for law enforcement agencies. Victimized families bear a heavy burden of stress that keeps blood pressure abnormally high due to their males being targeted.[37] Many are worried that fathers, sons, brothers and husbands may one day be murdered by police officers convinced of racist stereotypes.

In maintaining the racial status quo many Euro-Americans dismiss as trivial the complaints of African-American males directed at law enforcement officers.

Many regard such complaints as a function of what author Norman Podhoretz once described as "paranoid touchiness".[38] But recent police assaults—one fatal— on two Negroid race immigrant males in New York City forms a distinct contrast between perception and reality.[39] It is a contrast that permeates media as a major force in the perception, and thus inferiorization, of African descended Americans.

Prior to the age of technology, print media was the primary vehicle for communicating information. What people could not learn by word-of-mouth was left to what they could learn by reading, or what the literate could read to them. Although print was an established media, it was largely informal and unregulated, allowing rationalization of the racist stereotypes of African-American males by unscrupulous profiteers. Such is evident in the 1996 New York case referred to as the Central Park Jogger.[40]

Late one evening, an upper, middle-class investment banker was taking her daily jog through New York City's Central Park. The victim--a Euro-American female--was violently attacked and raped. The theme was old, familiar, and too often sensationalized by the media who incited frenzy around the case by describing the accused inner-city youths as "animals" and a "pack." In an overt act of racism, the print media managed to make the point of the perpetrators racial identity via subtle implication and photography. Although this was not the first or last case of its kind in New York, it was a major story for local newspapers around the country. It was as if a message was being sent that the threat of these inferior-race males was real and indeed unexaggerated despite the fact they were later found incident via DNA evidence.

The ability of print media to misrepresent African-American males has no doubt had quite an impact on how they are perceived. That impact has only increased with the use of photographic technology. The camera has the ability to freeze a recognizable, detailed likeness of a person. Still motivated by profit, print media has used lighting, pose, attire, etc., to create whatever racist stereotype it deems appropriate. The alleged defendants in the case of the Central Park Jogger were photographed in lighting that further darkened their skin and the solemn expressions on their faces made guilt seem all the more believable.[41]

In perhaps the trial of the century, a darkened photo of O. J. Simpson appeared on the cover of *Time* magazine as an even more dramatic illustration of media racism. While it is debatable as to why the media portrays racist stereotypes, what cannot be disputed is the fact that too many African-Americans are characterized, regardless of demography, by such racist images not applied to their Euro-American counterpart.[42]

Since the advent of cable television, virtually every home across America has access to its programming. More so than print and radio, television is intimate. Its ability to drive home the stereotype of the African-American male was politically exploited, during a presidential election year, in the person of Willie Horton.[43] Mr. Horton had been let out of prison where he had been incarcerated for rape. There was nothing new about this old stereotype, but television allowed viewers to "pseudoexperience" Mr. Horton. It was assumed that citizens, both male and female, would then go out and vote accordingly. At any rate, George H. W. Bush, whose election team had exploited the image, did in fact win the 1988 presidential campaign.[44]

In a subsequent 1990 incident in Boston, Massachusetts, another African-American male was accused of murdering Mrs. Stuart, a pregnant, Euro-American housewife. The entire nation presumed the guilt of the accused, Mr. Bennet, based on media hype and its larger-than-life photographs of the murder scene. Only after an accomplice involved in the frame-up came forth to reveal that the husband was the murderer, was Bennett --the alleged African-American perpetrator --released from police custod.[45] The belief that Bennett was guilty as charged was arguably, in large part, a reaction to his race.

A more recent and dramatic manifestation of the racist stereotype perpetrated by mass media was the 1995 case of Susan Smith of Union, South Carolina. Smith, later convicted of murdering her two children, initially testified that she had been attacked by an African-American male. In the aftermath, this unknown assailant was presumed to have drowned her young sons and escaped with her car. Well aware of the stereotype, Smith assumed that the all-too-believable image of the African-American male would go unquestioned by her Scottsboro-like Southern town. Fortunately, police were not so reluctant to question the case. Their investigation led to the arrest and conviction of the Smith. Lost in the account of what had occurred was the fact that an African-American had, once again, been cited as the culprit in the crime. The major mass media headlines emphasized the drowning of two children while ignoring the indictment of an entire group of innocent citizens. Thus, while race by various media is regarded as socially irrelevant and constitutionally illegal, among African-Americans it determines their overall quality of life. It is a biologically irrelevant tool of oppression as a manifestation of the Atlantic slave trade, the antebellum and the pseudo-scientific rhetoric of past and present racists.

II

The Atlantic Slave Trade

Negroid races of Africa were the focus of the Atlantic slave trade. Slavery in general was not limited to any particular race or nationality, as both Africans and Europeans labored under bondage during the Mediterranean middle-ages. What is more, according to Thomas, African slaves had been dispersed throughout North Africa and parts of the Mediterranean for centuries.[1] Most were derived primarily from Ethiopia, hence in fifteenth-century terminology African slaves, regardless of their origin, were referred to as "Ethiops".

As Islamic factions began to assume and expand their power in West Africa during the middle-ages, the trade in slaves spread north to the Sahara. Their barter was much in demand as servants, soldiers, and field hands. Particularly among Islamics, African slaves were especially valued as eunuchs and civil servants. News of their utility spread throughout the world including Renaissance Italy, where African slaves worked in abundance. Still others were coerced to Spain and Portugal. Some went to Christian locations, such as the brotherhood known as "Los Negritos." As trade in human cargo increased, the Portuguese began kidnapping Africans in the latter part of the fifteenth century, when they could not barter for them during their trek down the West Coast of Africa. Their original objective was gold but, finding little, took to abducting African men and women. Once subdued Portuguese workers transported their human cargo to Lisbon where they were sold locally or shipped to Spain and Italy.[2]

Interest in African slaves grew rapidly given their reputation as able workers with strong backs capable of enduring intense heat. This made them ideal for hard work on sugar, coffee, or cotton plantations or in gold mines, and other hostile environments. In addition, as people, they were assumed to have been laughable, good-natured workers who were quite docile. In their homeland many had been workers in agriculture and cattle interests. By comparison, Native-Americans and Europeans were considered a weaker sort. For this reason, European slaves, many of whom lived in Spain, Greece, and the Balkans, never made it to the New World. Similarly, Africans who were Islamic could not be effectively controlled and many were at least as cultivated as their European masters.[3]

The method of capturing slaves was left to traders' creativity and ingenuity. No method was too cruel or inhumane, thus some captives were abducted via wars waged by the Portuguese for the sole purpose of profit. Others were apprehended as a result of the Africans' cooperation in selling those they might defeat in battle. It should be noted that the African version of slavery differed from that of the Portuguese and other Europeans. To Africans, a slave was one forced into servitude but one who remained a man nonetheless. To the Portuguese and other Europeans, the African slave was reduced to an animal without benefit of soul or conscience. Such was a brand of servitude and cruelty unprecedented in the history of mankind. Capture by any and all methods was the means by which the majority of African slaves arrived in the Americas.

In its dimensions of barbarity the European Atlantic slave trade was characterized as a disgraceful means of profit. The inhumane regard for laborers in general at the time left much to be desired, such as the ill treatment of sailors, soldiers, and indentured English laborers. However, all by far had been much less brutalized in comparison to their African counterparts. Those traders who wished to entertain some level of civility for themselves found ways to insulate themselves from the sufferings of their human cargo. They would consider murder, rape, and beatings as merely a cost of doing business. Many had been previously involved in other ventures, which put them in direct contact with the physical abuse of slaves and they consequently learned quite well to tolerate packed holds, the odor, the suffering, and the fears so common on every voyage to the dark continent.[4]

As a moral shame in the conscience of Europe, slavery weighed heavily. However, its necessity assured its continuation for the time being. Following the discovery of the Americas, Europe was willing to abandon its moral conscience for profit. In the settlement of the New World, a small group of selfish merchants and planters cooperated to bring about the wholesale development of African people as a means of personal wealth. Their efforts complimented slavery in Europe throughout the middle-ages, finding support among some of the most noble in society. Thus not only did profit-motivated merchants partake but so did kings and the upper echelons of society who were convinced that Africans were racially inferior.[5]

The belief in African inferiority has little basis in fact. The presumption of what is primitive and what is not may be given to subjective speculation, but to suggest that what is primitive is also inferior is self-serving.[6] For example, the cultures of the Ashantis, Fantis, Yorubas, Mandingos, Hausas, and Dahomey were arguably advanced and well developed. To assess people as being barbaric savages is tantamount to a serious distortion of fact. Long before the Atlantic slave trade, such groups evolved cultures that were sophisticated even by European standards. Thus, assessment of Africans as savage and barbaric is not a conclusion drawn from fact but from choice by Europeans who sought some means of justifying African enslavement.[7]

By the twelfth century most countries in northern Europe had abolished the business of trading in slaves. Despite their efforts slavery remained a course of action that was unopposed under the right circumstances. Conscientious nations were most amenable where migration to and settlement of the New World was concerned. Under such circumstances the brutality of the business seemed less urgent. Perhaps history had a role to play in the way such nations viewed themselves. After all, if Athens and other genesis sites of Western civilization employed slaves to build the great Parthenon, and Rome employed slaves to maintain the aqueducts, Europe could not be held morally accountable for employing slaves to help build the New World.[8]

The impact of the slave trade on the affairs of Europe was considerable. Conversely, slavery should not be viewed as anything primary or the motivating factor for any specific industry or movement. Some contend that the slave trade was indeed an impetus for Europe's industrial revolution, but their contentions are not shared by the mainstream. However, those who managed to acquire wealth by trading in slaves invested some of their profits to the benefit of Europe. For example: one trader invested in Portuguese journeys of discovery, another assisted in the financing of England's Sankey canal; still another was a pioneer of cotton manufacturing, etc.[9] Additionally, the slave was not removed from an impact on shipbuilding, marine insurance, the rope industry, carpenters, textile, guns, iron, brandy and rum, as well as sugar refineries.[10]

The active abduction of Africans from their homeland influenced the native population. The obvious decrease in their numbers was assumed to have been supplemented by a fertile populous. Those who had the misfortune of being captured, while reducing the overall numbers, would have been equaled or more than equaled by natural reproduction. Statistics at the time suggest that African women comprised little more than a third of the slaves who were captured. Historians contend that an actively increasing population could have been stabilized by the slave trade in population reduction as a way of sustaining available resources. They contend that the population of West Africa around the eighteenth century was calculated at 25 million. This would mean a growth rate of about seventeen persons per thousand every ten years. Subsequently, the impact of the slave trade would have been to compromise population growth given that the numbers of those destined for bondage was about equal to the numbers of natural increase.[11]

The items traded for slaves were of great importance to the slave traders. Those who did not exercise wisdom and good business acumen might find themselves at a severe loss. Therefore, they chose very carefully the objects they bartered for their human captives. Consequently, slave ships resembled floating market places to assure their ability to trade at various locations.[12] One item that enabled trading was cloth. Cloth was commonly exchanged for slaves at numerous ports in and around Europe. Africans were not very impressed with manufactured wool and cotton goods, but they did take to such untailored materials so as to wrap themselves with it.

As much as Africans enjoyed trading European goods for slaves, their 500 years of contact with Caucasians did not inspire Africans to idealize Europeans in any way. Some historians interpret this as a failure on the part of Africans, affecting what their state of civilization could have gained. Others would contend that the reluctance of Africans to idealize Europeans can be seen as a sign of strength in which the African personality found enough worth so as to have little need to submit to outside influences. Missionaries from Europe made considerable efforts to export religion, often to no avail as they could not inspire their African subjects. To appear morally secure some Catholic priests were critical of slavery, as were some Protestants. However, their objections in the wake of a need for African labor carried little influence where it mattered. Thus in England and other parts of Europe involved in the slave trade there was minimal opposition to slavery until the late eighteenth century. That opposition was induced by the abolition movement and the publication of significant literature that criticized slavery as an unethical and barbarous act. Among the most noted of Protestants were Quakers who themselves had been active in the slave trade and thus knew firsthand the cruelty it entailed. It is unlikely that the movement to curtail slavery would have been as successful were it not for involvement of the Quakers. They applied themselves to the organization of their own and others to influence the concept of slavery as an affront to all of mankind—not just to the Africans who were directly victimized.

Consequent to the abolitionist effort of Quakers Europe had begun to express disdain for slavery. Influential members of society employed their wealth and power in France, Britain, Spain, and elsewhere to bring an end to the practice. Engaging the press, government, and other networks, the morally conscious brought an end to the Atlantic slave trade in both Europe and the Americas. Historians note that slavery came to an end not for practical business reasons but due to the work of activists such as Quakers who invested both time and energy to make it happen. They also cite notable individuals, such as Thomas Clarkson in England, Moses Brown in the United States, and Benjamin Constant with his French influence.[13] Others include Dom Pedro of Brazil, which is now home to the largest African descended population in the Western hemisphere.[14] Not all would welcome the actions of the aforementioned with admiration. Britain's involvement in the abolitionist movement was viewed by some as an example of British aggression and arrogance pertaining to the affairs of sovereign nations. Despite such behavior Britain's role in the abolition of the Atlantic slave trade was critical and more than atoned for any acts of arrogance.

Once the Atlantic slave trade ended, the freeing of those who had made the journey by ship across the Atlantic did not happen. In fact, it is likely that in some form those in America who had accumulated enough wealth could find ways to supply themselves with additional slaves from abroad. The rationale was that Africans were necessary to process cotton and sugar crops, which involved work Euro-Americans could not do. Many in America considered the harsh sun and otherwise hostile environment for slaves to be their natural element. They insisted that God had created Africans for the sole purpose of such work to enable the evolution of Western civilization via their ability to thrive in such harsh conditions. Without the African, America today might be little more than the vast wilderness it was when "discovered" by Columbus. Nothing could be further from the truth. In fact, with the arrival of Europeans to the New World, Africans were not available as slaves in any significant numbers to attend to its labor needs. Euro-American farmers labored in the fields planting cotton and doing other hard work under hostile conditions. Also, Euro-American women in Mississippi and Alabama were not averse to working in the hot sun whenever they were needed. The fact is Africans did not thrive any better than Caucasians in the harsh conditions of the New World. The difference was attributed to the fact that Africans, unlike their free European counterparts could be coerced whether they were in a state to endure or not.

The association of power with privilege extends to the history of Africans in America and can be traced to the slave trade. Forced into bondage, native Africans crossed the Atlantic in slave ships to contribute in part to the New World population. Among slave traders were the Portuguese, who maintained ownership of most of the West African coast where present day African-Americans trace their racial heritage. The first exposure of these Africans to the New World came by way of Haiti, or what was then called Hispaniola. These African slaves replaced Native American Indians to work in the mines, as Indians were not seen by slave traders as being strong enough to endure the harsh labor. By approval of the Catholic Church, African slaves eventually replaced Indians entirely, given their assumed greater strength and stamina. Accordingly, in 1517 arrangements were made for a large contingent of slaves to be imported for purposes of strenuous mine work.

Following the Portuguese, Sir John Hawkins is regarded as one of the first Englishman who engaged in the slave trade. Word of his success was followed by participation of his countrymen who took slave trade activities to an unprecedented level. According to historians, between 1680 and 1700, the English abducted no less than 300,000 Africans.[15] By 1786, Jamaica alone had landed over 600,000 Africans.[16] However, more importantly for African-Americans, a Dutch ship traveled from the Guinea Coast to Jamestown, Virginia, in 1620 carrying a cargo of some twenty African captives. Their arrival at Jamestown began the history of slavery in the English colonies and what would eventually become the United States of America. All totaled by the end of European trade in slaves, approximately 12 million Africans had been uprooted from their homeland under the authority of forced bondage. An equal number, 12 million, were said to have perished in raids or the cruel conditions they were forced to endure by transport on ships destined for the Americas. The cruelty and inhumane conditions they experienced on slave ships packed with little more than breathing room was unprecedented then and until now in human history.

The living condition of slaves and treatment by their masters was contingent on the master's character, which under the circumstances was more often lacking. Despite the fact of the slave's cruel treatment, the various colonial settlements maintained some form of law to protect slaves from injury. The objective, however, was not one based on humanity, but was based on the protection of property. While the Catholic Church struggled with the treatment of slaves, other religious sects were more assertive. In Philadelphia, Pennsylvania, the Quakers prescribed explicit objections to the barbarous and ruthless treatment of Africans who found themselves the victims of human bondage. Astonishingly, in 1776, the Quakers of Philadelphia declared that any among its membership who held slaves must free them immediately. Other conscientious groups formed abolition societies to oppose and otherwise prevent American participation in the slave trade. Finally, after much opposition and debate on trafficking in slaves, the British Government forbade the importation of slaves into the colonies by law in 1805.[17] In 1808, the United States followed Great Britain in its decision to discontinue the importation of slaves.[18] However, it should be acknowledged that while the importation of slaves to the New World was illegal it continued secretly and unlawfully until and during the American Civil War. Eventually, the slave trade was outlawed in South America and all the states of Europe.

While trading in human cargo was outlawed, the institution of slavery was firmly established at the time of the American "Declaration of Independence," in 1776. What is more, it had been ratified by the Constitution in 1788. By then, a million or so slaves had been settled in the U.S. colonies. It is significant to note that while slavery had began to decline in the North, it became a way of life in the South where dominant group privilege was tied to human bondage. The North was thus in a position to claim a moral high ground where dependency on slavery might be an option. The South, likely no less moral, relied on slavery to support its economy and for this reason used every means available to justify it. The issue of slavery became a source of tension between the North and South that culminated in the Civil War. In the aftermath of war between the northern and southern states, slavery was then brought to an end not for reasons of humanity but in an effort to preserve the Union. On 1 January 1863, President Abraham Lincoln introduced the "Emancipation Proclamation" to Congress, which legally ended the institution of slavery in the United States.[19]

Belief in the racial durability of Africans was necessary because Europeans both at home and particularly in America desired such exploitation. Given the notion that by race Africans were genetically fitted to do hard work their enslavement could be rationalized as a natural order of the biological universe. In addition, it was assumed that Africans, in comparison to those of other races—especially Europeans—possessed biological attributes that uniquely qualified them to be the property of Caucasians.[20] In the American South this belief was the beginning of the nation's tenacious "race problem" and prompted what would be necessary religious, social, and scientific efforts to justify bondage.

When Africans and Europeans first encountered one another in the South and colonial America their cultural differences were an obstacle to the assimilation process. Their striking physical contrasts made this an issue for centuries. That Africans and Europeans spoke different languages was insignificant in that each used speech as the primary means of communication.

Their mutual value for labor, the family, and governance made for a commonality however much they may have differed in detail. Their sense of ethics may have departed somewhat, but they also agreed. Moral versus immoral, bad versus good, and a general sense of right and wrong established the potential for Caucasoids and Negroids to cooperate short of a practical reason to do otherwise. Also, both were intelligent beings who possessed the talent and skills to advance their group. These attributes were not distributed by race but throughout humanity in toto .[21]

In the aftermath of Europe's moral attack on slavery, Americans could not effectively deny that slavery was wrong. The need for slave labor in the South was no less urgent, but there was less tolerance motivated by abolitionists who were becoming more daring in their attempts to eliminate it completely. In an effort to maintain their way of life, Euro-American Southerners increasingly sought the support of science to substantiate race as a valid concept in the hierarchy of humanity. Given the efforts of scientists, the race arguments quickly gained momentum. Nineteenth-century doctors, and pseudo-scientists-phrenologists of all sorts and backgrounds amassed a considerable following.[22] They were credited with having discovered scientifically a physiological basis for the temperamental and intellectual differences between Caucasian race groups and their inferior Negroid counterpart. The distinguished Dr. Samuel W. Cartwright, of Louisiana, took the position that "the visible difference in skin pigmentation also extended to the membranes, the muscles, the tendons, and . . . [to] all the fluids and secretions."[23] Even more astounding was Dr. Josiah C. Nott, of Mobile, Alabama, who insisted that not only were Africans, i.e., Negroids who were significantly different from Caucasoids, but that both belong to entirely different species.[24] Thus was born a new and virulent form of African inferiorization that would have an indelible impact on the American social conscience and sustain the Caucasian status quo vis-à-vis race.

The incorporation of science in support of African inferiority was not localized to America. Though much less pronounced during the time of the

Spanish-American War, the "white man's burden" was applied as justification for worldwide Caucasian imperialism.[25] Among noted scholars on the topic were John Fiske and John W. Burgess. It was their contention that Caucasians, Anglo-Saxons in particular, were superior to all other races of mankind. Their counterpart, Professor Ulrich B. Phillips, in 1918, rationalized the enslavement of Africans by professing that Negroids "by racial quality" are "submissive," "light-hearted," "amiable," "ingratiating," and "imitativ"[26] Consequently the abduction of Africans from their native land to bondage in America had no more effect on his racial predispositions than it did on his dark skin.[27] Sometime following Phillips, an agricultural economist voiced considerable doubts as to whether it was slavery during the antebellum that caused Africans to be stereotypically incompetent, inefficient, and irresponsible workers. Not to assign such ignorance to men during the infancy of science is the fact that, as recently as 1953, Caucasian scientists commented similarly. One distinguished biochemist took the position that the races of mankind, "like breeds of dogs, may possess distinctive emotional characteristics, and that the Negro's inborn temperament may have made his enslavement feasible."[28]

Being of such recent tenure, the pseudo-scientific rhetoric of American scientists have become a mainstay in the justification of African-American oppression. In fact, few among African-Americans today count their ancestors solely from among those who arrived via the Atlantic slave trade. They are in actuality the descendents of Native- and Euro-Americans as well as Africans. Their racial heritage is more accurately a combination of Negroids, Mongoloids, and Caucasoids. Additionally, while Africans are indigenous to Africa, the Negroid composition there is a combination as well. Hence, while slaves for the most part arrived from the coastal areas of West Africa, many hailed from Central Africa, South Africa, East Africa, and Madagascar, including Bantus, Bushmen, and Hottentots. While all were dark-skinned and of kinky hair by Caucasian standards, their phenotypes differed significantly from the scientific characteristics assigned to Negroids in general.[29] Astonishingly, none of the distinguished scientists who referenced racial issues expressed any concerns for this otherwise obvious contradiction to their gross generalizations.

The rationale for inferiority of Africans was not limited to science. Religion, i.e., Christianity, was instrumental in suggesting that the "Creator" of mankind had destined the African-American for Southern bondage, which was attributable to ancient sins. Thus Christian mythology contributed to the belief in African inferiority evident in the depiction of Negroid people. By cultural myth extended from biblical tales, Africans had been effectively demonized. The most noted of such tales is that of Ham. According to Christian tradition, Africans are descendants of Ham, the son of Noah. As the story goes, Ham was to have looked on his father naked—a strong sexual implication. As punishment for this indiscretion, God was said to have willed that Ham's son and all his descendants would be "black."

The association of Africans with Ham provided a convenient mechanism for accusations of their rejecting paternal authority by Western commentators. The blackening and rejection of Ham's descendants then represents—according to Christian mythology—the retaliatory castration by the higher Father in God. As per Freud's psychoanalysis, what is "black" and/or banished would not be seen, as when King Oedipus was said to have blinded and banished himself for learning of what he had done. After punishing one among their number, Noah's remaining sons then earned the approval and protection of God, their paternal Father. This scenario represented cultural absorption of the superego by the West. It furthermore contributed to the belief in racial inferiority. The bad and evil son, set apart from humanity by the curse of "black" skin, had been forever banished from the acceptable fold of humanity until the European descendants of Noah discovered him again, in Africa.[30]

In more modern times Western scholars sought to scientifically rationalize the story of Ham. One of their first attempts to account for "black" skin was saying that the color was due to the intense sun in the African region. This hypothesis did not last very long considering that there were Native-Americans on a similar latitude in the New World who, by comparison, were quite light-skinned. In the minds of the most learned among men, the myth of Ham was utilized to account for what could not be substantiated scientifically. Subsequently, it became suitable for Europeans, enabled by psychodynamics, to inculcate the view that the bodies of Negroid peoples were a manifestation of the most primal of curses among mankind. These assumptions formed the bases for the many fantasies surrounding race. However, early on such fantasies had yet to be applied to an abstract concept of race per se, but they did encourage justification for slavery and notions of the "white man's burden." The eventuality of an Atlantic slave trade and Western colonization brought about fantasies pertaining to blackness associated with African people, which grew in intensity and culminated in racial mythology. Thus, as per Freudian psychoanalysis, among civilized nations in Europe and elsewhere, Negroid race people—Africans in particular— represented the embodiment of filth and disgust.[31]

Freud's psychoanalysis of inferior races is motivated by the super-ego. The ego designated the id (something not seen) as being associated with darkness, i.e., "black." Thus, the id represents blackness within the personality. Its underlying components, repressed from consciousness, reveal themselves symbolically vis-à-vis fantasies of race.

In Freud's psychodynamics of blackness Western civilization has revealed by way of projection how it has acted on the revelation of African people. Christianity has assumed the task of being a direct representative of the culture that destroyed African civilization, necessitating among Africans the need for missionary assistance. Its dual role makes it an appropriate sacrifice, in the blackness myth, to the more barbaric entity that it serves. Thus, having wedged itself securely into the Western psyche, race via Africans dominates as the focus of inferiority. Psychodynamically, Western culture has found a way to resolve—

through projection—many racial conflicts at the expense of Negroid people. It was a convenient justification for slavery. Vis-à-vis the concept of race, the European slave trader was psychologically free—that is, without guilt—to exploit Africans as was presumed necessary. This allowed for the unconscious Oedipal symbolism without inhibition to be acted out in real life: the antebellum maternal figure is divided into the pure "white" mother and the impure, lustful "black" "mammy." The African-American male represents divided roles of the bad father to be castrated and the bad son—Ham—to be castrated as punishment vis-à-vis his father (Noah). He is also the end of projected Oedipal desires for the antebellum "white" mother. The "black" woman becomes a sexually available object for repressed "white" Oedipal desires for the mother while, at the same time, symbolizing lust.[32]

The psychodynamic of projection is not without consequences to the African-American male and Euro-American psyche. The situation ultimately deprives Euro-American women of full maternal and sexual gratification. For some African-American males there is self-hatred and passivity. The highly sexualized ritual of Southern slavery is obvious in its preoccupation with the African-American rapist of Euro-American women, castration as punishment during lynchings, and sexual exploitation of the African-American woman—not to mention exaggerated religiosity.

In the aftermath of the antebellum era, a new form of racial inferiority has emerged in the manifestation of aversion. The previously omnipotent Southern "white" slave owner had created a situation where he could act out his Oedipal fantasies and conflicts free of consequence. The African descendants of slaves have now become the very symbol of these atrocities and, in polite circles, something to be avoided in conversation. Christian scholars continue to support that effort. Psychodynamically it follows that Southern—and Northern— segregation is regarded as a shift from an id-dominated slave culture to an ego-dominated one, giving way to a clean, rational, hard-working, and

self-controlled citizen. Their penchant for projection victimizes Negroid people—
African-Americans in particular—as an adversary. By definition of race they are
presumed to be dirty, emotional, lazy, and lacking in self-control, especially
where sexuality is concerned. This more subtle form of racial inferiority is evident
in the need for a civil rights movement, affirmative action, and other modern day
efforts.

Consequent to Christian mythology, Africans as members of the Negroid
race were effectively characterized as barbarians who required the constant
discipline and control of their European masters. Their enslavement was a
necessity in order that they be rescued from themselves to enable Western and/or
Caucasoid civilization. According to South Carolina's code of 1712, Africans
were "of barbarous, wild, savage natures, and . . . wholly unqualified to be
governed by the laws, customs, and practices of this province."[33] They were
meant instead to be governed by special laws "as may restrain the disorders,
rapines, and inhumanity to which they are naturally prone and inclined, and [as]
may also tend to the safety and security of the people of this province and their
estates."[34]

Exactly how colonial South Carolinians viewed this assumption privately
is not readily apparent. However, what is apparent is that even today the best
among them see African peoples as lacking in civility for whatever reasons. They
feel for the most part that African slaves were primitive and could only advance
beyond their station in life by acquiring European culture as a vehicle to civility.
One historian of note referred to the plantation as "a school constantly training
and controlling pupils who were in a backward state of civilization. . . . On the
whole the plantations were the best schools yet invented for the mass training of
that sort of inert and backward people which the bulk of the American Negroes
represented."[35]

There is little doubt that when Africans arrived in America they had
difficulty navigating their new environment and its unfamiliar institutions, but the

belief that they needed to be civilized was not based in truth. In fact, the first generation of Africans born in America during the seventeenth century were equally prepared for Western civilization as were those freed by the later "Emancipation Proclamation."[36] The process of acculturation and civilization was not contingent on race but on experience and education. Thus, only by living as equal citizens could Africans in America be expected to assume their place as law abiding and productive members of society. The plantation system had as its goal the objective of ensuring that did not happen.

African-Americans today are the descendents of people and cultures that were superior in many ways to those in Europe before and during the Atlantic slave trade. Some had developed an agricultural economy that rivaled the complex organization of the later plantation system. The crops they harvested necessitated specific tasks to be performed by men and women in association with a complex scheme in division of labor. They were joined by skilled craftsmen who played significant roles in the overall society. Consumers negotiated for goods and services via an exchange of monetary mediums. Other institutions equaled the monetary system in complexity. No doubt it was in fact due to the relative sophistication of some African cultures that Europeans were inclined to enslavement of the people. Nomadic peoples, regardless of race, could not have successfully met the labor challenges of Western civilization.[37]

Given the Southern, Euro-American need for the slave system, Caucasians grew more obsessed with the racial denigration of African-Americans. The visual differences in pigmentation between racial groups exacerbated the notion of Negroid inferiority that was being peddled by racist scientists. Thus, by the nineteenth century, the prevailing assumptions about African-Americans were based on such superficialities and dominated culture, institutions, religion, science, and the mindset of the American populous. To the contrary, no one could scientifically substantiate that the racial attributes of African-Americans accounted for their believed fitness for bondage. As a result, no scientist of any note has been able to yet demonstrate with any degree of certainty that African-Americans are racially inferior or otherwise uniquely fitted for any forms of servitude.[38] That being so, scientists in the modern era such as biologists, psychologists, sociologists, and anthropologists contend that Caucasians and Negroids are equal. Their potentials for intellect, culture, and civilization cannot be differentiated on the basis of racial characteristics. In fact the concept of race is being increasingly challenged by all but the ignorant. This has created a source of embarrassment for racists who operate under the cloak of science.[39] While they labor less successfully than in years past they have not lost in an effort to sustain the status quo by race. In manipulating the details of intelligence testing, scientists including Herrnstein and Murray have kept the suggestions of African-American inferiority viable. By attending to the existence of intelligence test differentials between the races, the question of racial inferiority encourages continued debate.

While there is some question pertaining to intelligence, the racial variations in personality traits are as inconsistent intra-racially as physical attributes. Consequently, it is then all but completely impossible to scientifically validate generalizations about races. This makes it plausible even to racists that Africans were no more suited for slavery than their European captors. Ultimately, enslavement was fitted to some Negroids and Caucasoids or none at all. Finally, the fact that there had been slaves who were Caucasian suggests that to infer some innate fit of Negroids for bondage was more political than scientific.

III

Race

Social environments--formal or informal, African-American or otherwise--can be neither understood nor assessed for their logic without a frame of reference. Slavery is the frame of reference for the significance of race. This is true for either the antebellum or the present era. The comprehension of race represents an effort to discover an otherwise concealed objective. It will illustrate with clarity the social environment of those victimized by racial oppression, extended from previous bondage and other forms of domination. It will characterize the secret notion of hierarchy manifested in quality of life education, occupation, and income levels. As frame of reference the study of race is not an attempt to criticize or pass judgment, but merely to serve as a mirror in which America can view a reflection of itself. In that way it can overcome some of the devastation of its past.

Variations in human physiology accommodated the Western invention of race. Race categories have dominated civilization as the differential crux of mankind.[1] Scholars differ as to the number and nomenclature of race categories, but included in the discussion are Negroids, Caucasoids, and Mongoloids.[2] Every ethnic and national grouping of human beings can be represented by one of these three categories. The first, or original man, as far as archaeologists are able to determine, was a member of the Negroid grouping. Negroids are indigenous to Africa and characterized by dark skin, coarse hair texture, and broad noses. Caucasoids and Mongoloids by physiology are much in contrast to the Negroid. In contemporary American categorization Negroid and Mongoloid race groups are referred to as "minorities," distinguishing them from Caucasoids.[3]

The genesis of race begins with the origin of man and is purely a matter of conjecture. As recorded in numerous history texts, human origin relative to earth's existence began quite recently. The first appearance of homo-sapiens was on the continent of Africa. Although the entirety of the continent is now inhabited, the southern region is thought to be the birthplace of human-beings.[4] According to Darwin, human-being as intelligent organism represents the final link in a succession of primates who would dominate earth. Whether one is inclined to accept this notion is arguably a matter of intellectual preference. However, few if any scholars will take exception to Africa as the location of human origin. Hence, every person alive today, whatever their so-called race, ethnicity, or native language, is at some point on the scale of human evolution the child of those descended from inhabitants of the "dark continent!"

The concept of race as applied to persons of African descent dates from the categorization of groups in the dawn of human history. Much of what has been studied and recorded historically is the product of Eurocentric perspectives. According to these perspectives the original African is regarded as the Bushman. The African-American, while related in many ways to the Bushman, likely came from regions of the African continent distant from the Bushman population. Their separation undoubtedly took place during a remote period in history. However, the chief divisions of the native population of Africa include the Bushman, and the Bantu who invaded South Africa, driving out the original Bushman. After centuries of invasion and various other forms of conflict it is difficult to ascertain any racial purity among those who would later come to be known as African-Americans.

In the opinion of biologists and medical personnel, race is scientifically meaningless. By reference in any number of English dictionaries this fact alone would define it as a myth. Scientists motivated by an earnest drive for knowledge contend that valid facts are one form of knowledge and myths are another. Facts should be the results of rigorous scientific methods, which seek truth without the imposition of ulterior motives. Myths, on the other hand, have no methods to which the scientist must adhere. The distinction between fact and myth is not necessary, given that myth is no more or less valued for its ability to facilitate truth as truth is not the objective. Although the earnest scientist will note the ambiguities existent in rigorous scientific findings, said scientist will also acknowledge the human limits of objectivity. Indeed, not every racially dominant Euro-American pursued the myth of race with reference to inferiority invigorated by notions of "white supremacy."[5] Some were quite fervent in their attempts to reach the truth. Unfortunately, such scientists were and remain limited by their exposure to misconceptions about racial precepts, which assured racial conclusions despite efforts to conduct research independent of such. Ultimately, for different reasons, the efforts of Euro-American scientists teamed with supremacists validated notions of race in sustaining race-based privilege and domination of so-called Negroids and Mongoloids as an oppressed underclass.

According to the latest research, any race in comparison to any other will reveal as much genetic diversity within each as between the two. When questioned about what race is the objective, scholars will contend that the concept of race is a fallacy.[6] Yet race forms a substantial part of American ideology. It is illogical and in many instances self-contradictory. To the contrary, when social scientists are questioned about what race is all will agree that while race may have no medical or biological significance it is no less a social fact. What then is the purpose of race if it has no medical or biological significance? At the turn of the 21st century, why has race remained ever potent as a source of heated debate among scholars and laymen alike?

Being germane to the American conscience, the concept of race commanded immeasurable attention. As a result, scholars of various disciplines began to ponder its validation. They invented nomenclature and theories to qualify it as a universal attribute of mankind thus ensuring its significance. Such luminary figures as Franz Boas devoted their entire careers to challenging the explanation and dissemination of race information. They had a profound influence on the work of African-Americans, including Booker T. Washington, W.E.B.

DuBois, and University of Chicago sociologist Robert Park. These scholars in turn influenced the careers of succeeding African-Americans, including E. Franklin Frazier, Horace Cayton, and Charles S. Johnson. Boas's unusual effort to challenge race theories inspired denigrated races to study the history and cultures of their forbears in more depth. This moved DuBois and others to document African history and culture and the contributions of Africa to civilization.[7] Much of the information had been ignored by mainstream scientists whose objectives were bound by the status quo, but ultimately the work of DuBois and others would reveal the notions of race for what they were: fallacies and contrived mechanisms for the oppression of non-Europeans.

In the opinion of conservative William Julius Wilson, author of *The Declining Significance of Race*, while race exists as a social fact its importance is on the decline.[8] To the contrary, race remains a potent myth of social construction: no more or less. It is utilized as a means to perpetuate institutional and personal forms of dominant race privilege. Such group privilege cuts across a multitude of categories including class, gender, sexuality, religion, ethnicity, etc. Unequivocally, race privilege gained legitimacy via science, which puts members of Caucasian groups in a position of domination over African- and other non-Caucasian-Americans without it ever being a formal element of strategy. The historical ascendancy of Europe validated the Caucasian scholar, scientist, missionary, and soldier because they could study, experiment, indoctrinate, and conquer with less than formidable resistance from those they deemed to be inferior races.[9] Under the guise of objective science and the tacit assumption of racial superiority there emerged a non-Euro typology suitable for study in the academy, display in the museum, for theoretical and anthropological analysis which put Caucasians at the zenith of the biological hierarchy. In its aftermath was the necessary invention of "white supremacy." Suffice it to say that while race has no biological significance, it is simultaneously a nonexistent social fact and a potent social construct. That is, since Americans continue to act on race as biological fact, the aftermath enables a host of real life advantages. These advantages in the context of privilege are attributed to dominant group power. By virtue of such power, the social "fact" of race and other fallacies are then subject to racial interpretation, making them never transparent and all but unchanging for those who immigrate.

Certain flora and fauna differ markedly due to variety and breed, hence in the purposes for which they are bred. Although almost any animal can be trained when young to perform some useful act for their owner, no owner would try to train a horse to tend sheep or retrieve rabbits. Similarly, the differences between draft horses and race horses, which are certainly conditioned in part by their heredity, accommodate the various functions decided by their master. The differences in horses have been selected by their masters via deliberate breeding processes. These breeding processes have been designed with particular functions for the animal in mind. By analogy, certain scientists have attempted the same process for human beings as a rationale for differentiations in intellect based on their race group category. These scientists contend that if race group category is amenable to the evolutionary breeding process then differentiations among races in their intellectual capacity is logical. However, their logic is not commensurate with the natural laws of biological heredity. For among human beings, as opposed to animals, what is inherited is not the issue, but the issue is the manner in which human beings respond to their environment. No doubt the amount and kind of human traits are determined by hereditary makeup. For example, human beings who carry the genes for blue, green, or brown eyes have blue, green, or brown eyes regardless of their environment. Eye color is rigidly fixed by biological and/or race group heredity. However, the color of skin as it pertains to race is not so rigidly fixed in biology, since it can change rather rapidly depending on the environmental exposure of the skin to sunlight. Finally, whether or not subjects perform well on standardized and/or IQ tests depends on their environmental socio-economic experience and exposure to the test. Human intelligence as defined by race-based criteria is, then, quite pliable and subject to change dependent on environmental conditions. Thus, in the interest of species survival human beings are almost always born with eyes of different color and an intellectual capacity to learn from experience.[10]

The idea that intelligence can be linked to racial constructs remains a compelling source of racism in modern day America. Due to the prestige of science, the merits of race as pertains to intelligence have been greatly exaggerated in the public mind. Many have been convinced that science, in the form of eugenics and other dominant group ideologies, has reached conclusions via the scientific method pertaining to things that have not been amenable to scientific inquiry. Motivated by self-serving interests, the most intelligent among them accept that science can provide measurement of things upon which scientists cannot even begin to agree on as to how to conceptualize. None question the role of race in determining the intellectual and artistic capacities of individuals based on their racial heritage. Consequently, standardized tests are assumed to assess these capacities despite the fact that race is a social construct and the definitive account of intelligence does not exist. This otherwise scientific absurdity has managed credibility in the mainstream of society that is contingent on little more than the forces of dominant group power. The bias of power is not new, but was used in recent American history to engage dominant group privilege, not on the basis of race but immigrant status.

Following the mass migration of Caucasian immigrants from Europe, America became populated by masses of immigrants who lived in poverty, were for the most part uneducated, and were confronted by an alien culture. After being tested many—though racially Caucasian--were determined by mainstream standards to be mentally defective. While test performance was no doubt impacted by familiarity with the English language and American cultural norms, American scientists insisted that recent immigrants from southern and eastern Europe had performed poorly on intelligence tests because they were members of inferior race groups. Inferior race groups included Jews and Slavs, who were assumed dull witted compared to Nordics who were assumed to be intellectually superior. Scientists explained away the obvious correlation between test scores and the number of years lived in America by insisting that the earlier immigrants were from northern Europe and Great Britain while most of the recent ones were from elsewhere. Noted scientist Carl Brigham headed the research effort while being celebrated in academic journals and other prestigious institutions for his work. That prestige was aimed at Congress to influence the direction of immigration restriction laws, which accommodated dominant group privilege. What is more, the same Euro-American scientist would eventually head the College Entrance Examination Board. That board became instrumental in the exclusion of African-Americans from higher education, based not on intelligence test performance but solely on race.[11]

Despite its fallacy, the concept of race in America remains controversial and charged with emotion. Activists from every institutional sector of society have found it necessary to insert their opinions for any number of reasons. Thus clergymen, anthropologists, and biologists have all contributed to what Americans know and think about race. However, it has been the input of social scientists, including social workers, psychologists, sociologists, etc. who have directed the prevailing conclusions. Their contributions and influence have taken on political implications, which further charge an already emotional issue. Certain scientific factions have taken it on themselves to advocate the "superiority" and "inferiority" of various race groups. By utilizing pseudo-scientific methods these so-called scientists have used race as a mechanism for the unfair distribution of wealth and maintenance of the dominant group status quo. No doubt, those presumed to be members of "inferior races" have sought to contest the meaning and significance of "race," and have often succeeded, but that success has never required little more than a minimum of effort given the obvious fallacy of racial constructs. Under the circumstances, it is logical to suggest that the continued prevalence of race is sustained by its commensurate association with power and dominant group privilege.

The association of race with slavery and dominant group privilege has sustained its impact in the 21st century. It remains a challenge to the present and future of America that will either give way to fascism or meet the demands of a multiracial democratic society. Liberal social scientists in particular cannot make their case alone. They are in fact more often constrained by their relative lack of influence in an era dictated by conservative ideology. Thus, at every opportunity the case must be made against racial constructs. Beyond the limits of ideological labels scholars must convince society of the inherent absurdity of race-based constructs. That is, scholars must make the case of race for what it is, a dominant group phenomenon invented for economic and political purposes. Notwithstanding, social scientists and other scholars have readily accepted the idea that racial constructs can and do have real effects on society. To the extent of having consequences, illusions and fallacies must then be reckoned with. Be it fallacy or not, the consequences of race requires an understanding of what it is about, to whom is it beneficial, to what end does it serve, and what are its parameters of resulting privilege. If one thinks of race as something contrived in part for dominant group privilege, then the idea of its existence is less confusing. Thinking of race as a privileged Euro-American social construct will reveal the key to its longevity, for inherent in the practical application of any social construct is a shelf life that exceeds every real life commodity. Hence, the shelf longevity of race is attributed to its function in sustaining Euro-American group domination of African-Americans by virtue of racial criteria.[12]

The challenges to race were significant in that they gave activists the means to confront disparities in the racial order. In particular, the study of social structures and class systems refuted belief in race as rationale for the economic and social conditions of Negroid race, i.e., African-American peoples. Due to the influence of Boas and his intellectual offspring, race could not go unchallenged as the dominant factor in social problems associated with second class races. Debates were spurred by intellectuals who embraced different interpretations of Boas's work as to whether class or race was the more potent dynamic in American race disparities. Regardless of the end result, even the challenging of race as a valid concept kept it forever in the conscience of the populous and thus at the forefront of its agenda. In a myriad of ways this American obsession with race is the mainstay for the continued oppression and victimization of minority race groups referred to as racism.[13]

Consequent to the belief in scientific racial differentiations, racism has prevailed as one of the most devastating and tenacious social problems in modern day America.[14] Volumes of literature have contributed little in bringing about its demise. Germane to the American version of racism is what transpires between African- and Euro-American citizens. Other people of color suffer similarly to the extent of their darkness in color. This is known as the black/white dichotomy. The black/white dichotomy by definition is predicated on the notion that racism manifests as discrimination by Euro-Americans, particularly against people of color.[15]

Racism as defined in social science is regarded as an extension of "white supremacy."[16] Scholars of the social sciences study in great detail the implications that result in various forms of racism. They trace the origins of drug addiction, hypertension, stress, family disruption, and other societal ills among minority race groups to its existence.[17] In some form it is a social fact as old as civilization itself. However, in a historical context its analysis as a tool of oppression is relatively recent.[18] Among Negroids and Mongoloids racism is the direct result of Caucasian domination. Following the Atlantic slave trade and Western colonization, Europeans evolved a racial hierarchy. The uppermost in status became those designated as Caucasian, superior, and destined to dominate other races by virtue of said superiority.[19] Dominated, and in an effort to assimilate, so-called inferior race groups have been imposed on by a value system that is in many ways not only racist but pathological. For a population as diverse and heterogeneous as that of Negroids and Mongoloids, the effort to assimilate without recognition of the existence of racism could prove counter to their mental health. It could impair the ability of a segment of the American population to value itself.

In a sociological context, racism, according to Banton,[20] refers to the efforts of a dominant group to exclude a dominated group from sharing in the material and symbolic rewards of society. It differs from other forms of exclusion in that qualification is based on race and its observable physiological attributes. Such attributes are taken to suggest the inherent superiority of the dominant race group, which is then rationalized as a natural order of the biological universe.[21]

The most zealous proponents of racism in America profess that Anglo-Saxon/Teutonic people are superior to other races as a matter of biological fact.[22] They postulate that they alone have been uniquely endowed with the capacities necessary to bring about civilization. Their so-called "advancing civilization" was a cultural form of racism devoted to rationalizing the right of Caucasians to embark on a mission aimed at dominating their racial subordinates.[23] By way of conquest, slavery, and/or colonization, Caucasians eventually influenced every sovereignty of the known world. In the wake of psychological justification, the mission to civilize "inferior" races necessitated a universal belief in the potency of race to elevate or taint.[24]

Racism in America is an embarrassing social problem.[25] At the root of its psychogenesis are dark-skinned, Negroid, African-American.[26] In an age of political activism and the rhetoric of diversity, Euro-American scholars have consistently paid less attention to its implications perhaps due to its embarrassing and explosive potential. Notwithstanding, to rank racism as anything less than a priority could result in dire consequences for the population as a whole. It will enable the perception of hierarchy within a single species and, in fact, provide a conduit for the continued social, economic, and political oppression, perpetuated on the basis of race at home and abroad.

In a society that has grown increasingly diverse in recent years there are many victims of racism. Included are Negroid race groups such as Latino- and African-Americans, and Mongoloid race groups such as Latino-, Asian-, and Native-Americans. All, to some extent have been victimized as a result of their inability to conform to Caucasian race criteria.[27] However, those of African descent have no doubt been the most victimized and despised in the wake of a racist legacy. Their subjection to the violent and brutal nature of bondage is without parallel in recorded human history. Racism extended from race is tenacious and omnipotent in American life. It has also victimized other racial groups in the relocation of Native Americans to reservations, the abuse of Latino-Americans who happen to be undocumented, as well as the more historically recent confinement of Asian-Americans to WW II internment camps. Hence, there is little doubt that racism, extended from race, that is left unchallenged will only intensify and become more pervasive in the future.

In any multiracial society that is not totalitarian, certain groups necessarily dominate others, just as certain movements are more influential than others; manifestation of this cultural tendency is recapitulated by racial constructs. The dynamics enabling it are compulsory to the comprehension of American culture in the modern era. It is racism, or rather the acting out of racism in America, that has contributed to the appeal and legitimacy of Euro-American group privilege. As an ideology, it is covertly associated with racism because it is an extension of male domination.[28] It necessitates an unspoken, collective notion of "us" against "them" among Euro-Americans. Furthermore, it is plausible that what made Euro-American privilege racist is the idea that being Caucasian is assumed to be superior to all other racial identities.[29] Extended from that belief is thus the subjugation of the non-Caucasian, i.e., the Negroid African-American. Additionally there is the racism of Caucasian ideas, which casts non-Caucasian people as beings of inferiority. Such ideas override the possibility that a more skeptical, independent thinker might conclude otherwise.

Most Euro-Americans will acknowledge, when pressed to do so, the socio-economic origin of racism in their country. They are quite aware that before the 15th century "discovery" of America, and before the slave trade, the world had little concern for racism. When Africans were assumed to be a sturdier lot and replaced Indians to work in the mines, the economic advantages of their bondage were just over the horizon. Shortly thereafter the totality of Western culture, religion, philosophy, and norms were summoned to justify racist institutions. After centuries of such racism, the phenomenon can now be studied as an event unto itself. Noted scholar W.E.B. DuBois supported the economic origins of race prejudice. However, he contends that in the longevity of economic privilege, given the exploitation of African-Americans, an American folklore gradually evolved. That folklore superimposed racism on the conscious determination of Euro-Americans to exploit African-Americans as means to a privileged way of life. This notion eventually sank into the depths of their subconscious, where it has become immune to their sense of justice. Thus, the fact that America is a racist society is no longer a moot issue.[30] Any number of groups commissioned to study racism during the 1960s have concluded that the root cause of African-American unrest is Euro-American racism. While African-Americans have known this for years, Euro-Americans having buried racism so far into their subconscious that they have lost the ability to confront it as a dominant mainstream. Fortunately, the groups they have commissioned to study it have decided to admit to its existence.[31]

Therefore, racism is not a mere political abstraction reflected passively by culture, scholarship, or its institutions. Nor is it representative of some nefarious plot to hold hostage and exploit African-American people. It is rather a distribution of political sensitivity into aesthetic, scholarly and race contexts. It is an elaboration not only of a basic racial distinction but a perspective.[32] By such perspective, scholarly discovery and/or philosophical reconstruction not only controls, but, in some cases, manipulates that which is manifestly different. It is otherwise a discourse that is by no means in a conspiracy relationship with Euro-American political factions in the raw, but is generated by an uneven exchange with various sources of power. Included, but not limited to, is political power, intellectual power, cultural power, academic power, and fact power. Indeed, racism does not represent the entire Euro-American body politic, and, as such, race has less to do with science than with mythology and worldly group co-existence.[33] By effectively linking race to intelligence, dominant Euro-American groups via power have fashioned co-existence with African-Americans to ultimately sustain the privilege status quo.

Lastly, in practice, racism involves much more than the actions and attitudes of an individual. It includes the group behavior of one race—in this case Caucasian Euro-Americans--that designates itself by race as the moral, social, and economic superior of all other races. Prejudices extend from this designation, which are supported and reinforced by the institutions they control. In the aftermath access to opportunity is limited to those of a single race group that sustains the Caucasian race status quo. Eliminating racism will therefore demand a personal investment and cultural effort to assess and accordingly invalidate race. America must commit itself to examining not only the ability of race in racism to assign unearned advantages to Euro-Americans, but also its ability to injure African-American and other minority race groups. If it cannot, the democratic ideals of the current republic will be no less denigrated than were the ideals of the emerging sovereignty.

IV

Quadroons, Octaroons, and Mulattoes

In an effort to denigrate African-Americans for being Negroid-race members, Euro-American "scholars" have historically called on science to validate their claims. When Americans consider race they are struck by the obvious physical differences. What scientists have attempted to do is explain those differences in the context of inferiority so as to rationalize the slave trade, antebellum, and, ultimately, white supremacy. Hence scientists have invested enormous efforts in the examination of race and racial combinations as the determining factors in the cultural, political, sexual, intellectual, and moral differentiations between the various race groups. In the aftermath it would appear that any differences in power and the current world order would be attributable to Darwin's survival of the fittest, those being of European/Caucasian descent.[1]

The issue of race was critical in the post-Atlantic slave trade and the antebellum periods. The effort to defend the lofty ideals of America during its infancy required a morally sound explanation to account for slavery and white supremacy. This was very important due to the fact that until the emergence of the slave trade Negroid populations had been regarded as superior to those located in harsher climates. They were described as exceptional in "wit and intelligence" resulting from an environment that "enlivened their temperament."[2] Thus, Rousseau continued early on to rhapsodize about the "Noble Savage."[3] Following the slave trade and industrialization of Caucasian populations it became necessary for purposes of needed labor to distinguish between those who would be enslaved and those who would enslave. Subsequently emerging from the "Noble Savage" were Africans who, by means of racial stereotypes, were immoral, ugly, dull-witted, and otherwise inferior to Caucasians.

In reducing Africans to animals, so-called scientists of the day produced considerable documentation. According to Hubbard, Allan Chase traces scientific denigration of African-Americans to the 1798 publication of Malthus's *Essay on Population*.[4] It is Chase's contention that Malthus's work emphasized class distinctions among Europeans. This contradicted those who suggest the work focused on distinctions between Caucasians and non-Caucasians including Negroids and Mongoloids. Additionally, Stephen Jay Gould traces the first scientific denigration of races to Linnaeus, who contended that Africans (Negroids) were "ruled by caprice," whereas Europeans (Caucasoids) were "ruled by customs."[5] What is more, with respect to morality, African men were lazy and African women were sexually bold, as evident in their lactation levels. Not by coincidence, Linnaeus and Malthus conducted their work following the Atlantic slave trade. While much of their research was racist, as Walter Rodney suggests, it is erroneous to think of Europeans having enslaved Africans for racist reasons. They did so purely for economic reasons in the needed labor supply to enrich Europe and the Americas. Successfully benefiting from African bondage required Europeans at home and in the Americas to validate this bondage in racist terms.[6]

Physicians, biologists, and others created rather sophisticated means of validating the bondage of Negroid people. They alluded to such measures as skull and brain size differentiations which they regarded as scientifically evident that Africans, by means of race, were inferior to Europeans. Those, such as Gould in the "Mismeasure of Man," give accounts of measurements exposing their obvious racial bias. In a more dramatic display, Gould also exposed bias in the work of respected French anatomist Paul Broca, who ignored those racial attributes that would have ranked Caucasians as inferior. His efforts documented the way in which Broca and his American counterpart, Samuel George Morton, modified their data until Caucasians were ranked as superior.[7]

Not to be outdone by the French, Dr. Samuel Cartwright, an American physician, authored *Diseases and Peculiarities of the Negro* in 1854. In this publication, then accepted as legitimate science, he contends that a deficiency in the "atmospherization" of the blood associated with a deficiency of brain matter was a problem that caused the Negroids of Africa to be unable to care for themselves.[8] In contrast to those who would excuse such absurdity as an historical error is the fact that it did not end over time. As recently as the 1940s Gunnar Myrdal, author of the classic *American Dilemma*, was amazed that the American Red Cross would not accept African-American blood during WWII. This form of racism eventually shifted to where African-American blood was eventually accepted, but only for exclusive distribution to African-Americans. The otherwise critical need for blood in a time of war was not enough to overcome the racist denigration of African people. Not until 1950 was the practice discontinued, as racial information was no longer required of those donating blood.[9] In addition, the irony is that the blood banking system was the invention of an African-American doctor, Charles Drew.[10]

Despite the efforts of so-called Euro-American "scientists," the idea that African-Americans were inferior as based on race could not be substantiated. Their failure has not influenced the discontinued use of race to categorize people. That categorization does not take into account that the concept of race has no biological significance. Because, as a species, human beings are relatively homogenous in their genetic makeup. If one so-called race were to cease to exist the species itself would not be terminated. This is because approximately 75 percent of human genes are the same. The remainder is known to exist in all groups, varying only by concentration. Given the level of human miscegenation over time it is safe to assume that the human gene pool is and perhaps always was fairly evenly distributed over all so-called races of man.[11]

Although the antebellum era institutionalized the idea of racial inferiority and white supremacy it did not discourage racial miscegenation, i.e., sex between Caucasian men and non-Caucasian women. While sexual contact between African-American men and Euro-American women was strictly forbidden a generation of mixed races emerged in the South that stood as testament to its moral lapses. Mixed races were no less oppressed than full-blooded African-Americans, but they experienced a different dynamic in the racial environment. Furthermore, the fact that race has no biological significance meant defining it was not possible. Hence scientists created the "one-drop theory" to define "mixed races" as "black." Therefore, anyone who was known to harbor even a trace of Negroid ancestry was designated as African. The fact that 90% of their ancestry may have been European and/or Caucasian was irrelevant. Suffice it to say that while race has no biological significance as per mixed-race Americans it is evidently a contrived tool of political, social, and other forms of oppression that have extended from White supremacy.

As the descendents of Euro-Americans, mixed-race groups were placed in an advantageous position within African-American society. Their Euro-American ancestry was sometimes advanced as evidence of the innate mental superiority of the Caucasian race. Others point out that the social premium on their light skin has induced many of the most able and successful among African-Americans to "marry light." Thus, a process of sexual selection has been going on for generations by which the mixed races have absorbed some of the best genes of the Negroid.[12] In addition to genetic advantages, the largest free African-American planters were almost always of mixed-race. Economic dominance allowed Euro-Americans to regulate the membership of the free African-American elite by determining who could buy land, open shops, or engage in certain trades.[13] Mixed-race African-Americans and others having light skin also brought a fancy price in the market; this may account in some part for the high percentage of mixed-race children produced on many of the slave-breeding plantations.[14]

The greater prestige of mixed-race African-Americans meant that the women especially were prone to a type of exploitation that those with dark skin did not encounter. It varied in certain areas of the country, but existed nonetheless. In some sections a sub-surface type of polygamy grew that approached an institutional form. Free mixed-race African-American girls became the mistresses of Euro-American men by whom they were supported and by whom they reared families of mixed-race children. In some cases these mixed-race mistresses and children were deserted, with or without income for their support, when the man married a Euro-American woman; in other cases the extra-legal relationship was continued and the family was supported in addition to the lawful household and the legitimate children. This type of dual family arrangement was particularly open and highly developed in New Orleans, Mobile, and certain other points of the Lower South.[15] The free mixed-race girls, whose families were frequently persons of some wealth and culture, aspired to such unions and, so long as there was hope of contracting one, scorned to marry with non-Caucasian or mixed-race men. Some of the pillars of American history are guilty of such moral lapses, including the respected Thomas Jefferson, the third president of the United States of America.

While this moral lapse could be expected of lesser men, it is widely held by serious scholars, such as Barbara Chase-Riboud and William Cobett, that Thomas Jefferson engaged for many years in sexual intercourse with a fourteen-year-old minor: a slave girl named Sally Hemings.[16] It is perhaps the most famous and controversial case of a Western "gentleman" keeping a "black" mistress. In this instance, Jefferson was an author of the "Declaration of Independence" and a historical legend.

According to Russell, Wilson, and Hall, in 1772, Thomas Jefferson married a widow named Martha (Wayles) Skelton, the daughter of John Wayles, a prosperous local plantation owner. Martha's father, a widower, kept a beautiful mixed-race slave named Betty Hemings. Shortly after Thomas and Martha's marriage, the slave gave birth to a daughter, Sally, who, in the context of slave culture, became Martha's illegitimate half sister. John Wayles died not long after Sally's birth, and Martha inherited 40,000 acres of land and 135 slaves, including Betty and Sally Hemings.

Jefferson's marriage to Martha was, by all indications, a happy one. They had six children together, although only two survived to adulthood. However, she suffered from poor health, had frequent miscarriages, and died after ten years of marriage at the age of thirty-three. At the time, Sally was nine years old and serving as Martha's personal servant. Jefferson was extremely distraught over his wife's death and turned to public service to escape his depression. He spent two years as a delegate to the Continental Congress and then, in 1784, he left for Europe, taking his two older children with him. After a year in London, he moved to Paris, where he served nearly four years as minister to France.

While in Paris, Jefferson received more tragic news from home. His second youngest child had died. Grief-stricken at losing yet another family member, he sent for his youngest daughter, Polly. An older slave who was supposed to accompany Polly on the long journey to Europe took ill, and a hurried decision was made to send Sally Hemings instead. Sally was then fourteen years old and showing unmistakable signs of burgeoning womanhood.

Some historians believe that Jefferson began having intercourse with Sally Hemings almost immediately after her arrival in Paris. One possible indication of his growing obsession with her can be found in his journal. Prior to her arrival in Paris, Jefferson used the word "mulatto" only once in forty-eight pages, but shortly afterward "mulatto" appeared eight times in fewer than twenty-five pages. He described even the countryside of Holland as "mulatto," a curious adjective for the highly literate Jefferson to employ about the landscape.

When he was preparing to return to America in 1789, Sally Hemings announced to Jefferson that she was pregnant, presumably with his child. At that point, she was forced to decide whether to accompany Jefferson back to America or to stay abroad. She would be free as long as she lived in France, but if she returned to America she would return to slavery. Jefferson allegedly persuaded her to return with promises of material wealth and the guaranteed freedom for her unborn child.

Back in America, about 1801, Jefferson was sworn in as the third president of the United States. Some believe that he and Sally Hemings were still sexually involved, after more than ten years since their return from Paris. She continued to live at Monticello, his Charlottesville estate, and over the years she bore five more children. Whether Jefferson fathered any or all of them became a source of national controversy. In an effort to sanitize his image, some biographic scholars have suggested that, in fact, the father of Sally Hemings' children was one of Jefferson's nephews, not Jefferson himself. A glaring contradiction to this disclaimer is that in his will, of all the slaves on his plantation, only Sally's children were allowed to go north to freedom.

A predominance of Western scholars have largely ignored the possibility that Thomas Jefferson may have engaged in sexual intercourse with a minor, and with a mixed-race Negroid minor at that. Perhaps they found it hard to believe that the same person who wrote, "all men are created equal" not only owned slaves but sexually exploited at least one of the children among them. Several decades passed after Jefferson's death before any of the evidence of this alleged liaison with Hemings was examined, and, by then, much of it had been lost or destroyed.

While many contemporary scholars refer to the story of this liaison as Jefferson's "alleged" affair, it is considered as fact for others. The story caught the attention of entertainers, such as Vanessa Williams.[17] Once the first African-American Miss America, Williams has wanted to take the story to Broadway as a serious play.[18] Steve Erickson and Barbara Chase-Riboud have both written novels about it.[19] According to recorded narratives, "at age 14, the war of my life had begun" and that adolescence is the end of innocence for female slaves. Few slave women had reached the age of sixteen without having been molested by slave-class males, on whose psyche the women's dark skin had a profound effect.[20] Once African-American men were shackled, the site of the battleground for white supremacy shifted, according to Stember, to the bodies of African-

American women.[21] The Hemings controversy finally inspired scientists to conduct DNA studies of Jefferson's descendants in 1998.

In an attempt to resolve the Jefferson controversy, genetic scientists Foster, Jobling, Taylor, Donnelly, de Knijff, Mieremet, Zerjal, and Tyler-Smith compared Y-chromosomal DNA from male-line descendants of Field Jefferson, a paternal uncle of Thomas Jefferson, with those of male-line descendants of Thomas Woodson, Sally Hemings' first son, and of Eston Hemings Jefferson, her last son. The molecular findings fail to support the belief that Thomas Jefferson was Thomas Woodson's father, but do, in fact, provide evidence that he was the biological father of Eston Hemings Jefferson.

It was in 1802 that the third president of the United States was first alleged to have fathered this "illegitimate" son of Sally Hemings.[22] The child was named Thomas by his mother and thought to have been born in 1790, shortly after Jefferson and Sally Hemings returned from France. Members of the Woodson family today believe that Thomas Jefferson was the father of Thomas Woodson, whose family name comes from his later owner. The family's claim however, has never been taken seriously by scholars, historians, or society, no doubt largely due to and because of its implications for the lack of morality at the highest levels of Western civilization.

Sally Hemings had at least four other children. Her last son, Eston (born in 1808), is said to have held a striking resemblance to Thomas Jefferson. As a result, he "passed" after settling in Madison, Wisconsin, as Eston Hemings Jefferson. Although his descendants believe that Thomas Jefferson was Eston's father, so-called Jefferson scholars give more credence to the oral tradition of the descendants of Martha Jefferson Randolph, the president's legitimate daughter. It is her contention that Sally Hemings' later children, including Eston, were in fact the offspring of either Samuel or Peter Carr, sons of Jefferson's sister, which would explain their resemblance to the president. Science, however, has ultimately sided with the descendants of Sally Hemings.

Apart from occasional mutations, genetic scientists have determined that most of the Y chromosome is passed unchanged from father to son. A DNA analysis of the Y chromosome can reveal whether or not individuals are likely to be male-line relatives. Therefore, those involved with the Jefferson study analyzed DNA from the Y chromosomes of five male-line descendants of two sons of the president's paternal uncle, Field Jefferson; five male-line descendants of two sons of Thomas Woodson; one male-line descendant of Eston Hemings Jefferson; and three male-line descendants of three sons of John Carr, grandfather of Samuel and Peter Carr. No Y-chromosome data were available from male-line descendants of Thomas Jefferson because he had no known surviving sons.

Four of the five male-line descendants of Thomas Woodson were proven unrelated, although they were characteristically Caucasian in origin. The fifth Woodson descendant was linked genetically to Africans. In contrast, the descendant of Eston Hemings Jefferson was genetically linked to Field Jefferson. The genetic materials of two of the descendants of John Carr were identical; the third differed only slightly. The Carr genetic material differed substantially from those of the descendants of Field Jefferson.

Conclusively, the findings of scientists Foster, et al., are that, while Thomas Woodson was not Thomas Jefferson's son, Thomas Jefferson, rather than one of the Carr brothers, was the father of Eston Hemings Jefferson. As a result, there can be no doubt by serious scholars that Thomas Jefferson, one of the most esteemed figures in American history, acted out what Bradley would refer to as sexual maladaptions of the Western male psyche.[23]

In a 1997 report by Dinitia Smith and Nicholas Wade, of the *New York Times,* the writers note that DNA tests performed on descendants of Thomas Jefferson's family and of his slave Sally Hemings offer new evidence that the third president of the United States fathered at least one of her children. According to their report, Jefferson, while almost fifty years of age, had taken advantage of a fourteen-year-old African-American female slave he owned. These findings again confirm an oral tradition that has been handed down among Sally Hemings' descendants for generations—that they are, in fact, also descendants of the third president of the United States.[24]

Antebellum males, like Jefferson, in particular longed to escape the confines of Christianity that equated sex with sin. Thus, the desire of Western males to abuse slave women extended beyond the breach of common men, but went to the very core of Western civilization. Antisocial sexual assault on mixed-race Negroid women was simply another way by which Caucasian males could be psychologically reaffirmed.

Regardless of whom they associated with mixed-race, African-Americans were not equal to the lowest of Euro-Americans. Variations in mixed-race were often designated in both public and private documents as follows: A Griffe was the offspring of a mulatto and a African-American; a mulatto was an offspring of a Euro- and African-American; a quadroon was from a Euro-American and mulatto; and an octoroon was from a Euro-American and quadroon. For convenience sake, the word mulatto was commonly used to refer to Americans of mixed-race, regardless of the variation and/or amount.[25] Since free African-Americans were never deemed equal to Euro-Americans, they created a society of their own. Within this group, class lines were just as tightly drawn as among Euro-Americans: the lighter the skin color, the higher the social position. Consequently, the Griffe looked down on the pure African-American; the mulatto regarded the Griffe as inferior and, in turn, was spurned by the quadroon;, while the octoroon refused any or little social intercourse with those racially below himself.

The view of American class structure is evidence of an advantage for mulattoes and gives a nucleus of a theory for the causal relations between income, wealth, occupation, and education on the one hand; and the integration of them to form a class system on the other. Overall, it is a matter of Negroid versus Caucasoid for the nation as a whole. Within the Negroid group, it is a matter of mixed-raced versus pure race, which gave the mulatto an advantage. The fact that they believed this wholeheartedly motivated them to work even harder. The differences in the lower-class,, who took a different view, were apparent. The income of this group was low and uncertain. High income, free mulattoes at one time did not accept their identity as African-American. The free mulatto families had generally formed the upper-class in the African-American group and often regarded themselves as an altogether different race. Some semblance of this tendency exists even today in cities such as Charleston and New Orleans. In the antebellum South, free mixed-race African-Americans were among the leaders not only in the economic life of the African-American population but also in the political and social life. This put them in a position to increase their income via the policies and laws that were adopted. Perhaps their newness and lack of political sophistication did not allow them to take full advantage. The failure to develop a substantial economic base for a middle-class hurt the professional groups in the African-American community which could be identified with the American middle-class. For this reason and others the association of mixed-race mulattoes with income in certain parts of the country may have begun to wane. Although in southern cities African-American society might continue to boast of Euro-American or mulatto ancestry, those in New York, Chicago, and Detroit were beginning to ask "what is his profession?" or "what is his income?"[26] Thus, although a mixed-race did not automatically secure an African-American's place in the hierarchy it often afforded him greater income opportunities.[27]

The mixed-race issue originated in the South, but it occurred elsewhere as well. African-American life in Philadelphia also found differences correlated to social class. There, African-Americans associated mixed-race with the so-called genteel tradition and hence with high status.[28] Those who are on the brink of status will go all out to appear to be a member. Income is lavishly spent on a home and on the education of children.[29] Those seeking entry into this genteel tradition willingly adopted its values especially where race was concerned. Thus, those at the top of the socioeconomic scale continued to be predominantly mixed-race while the race of those at the bottom was more Negroid by comparison.[30]

Lower-class African-Americans envied the status of upper-class mulattoes and were offended by their exclusiveness, while the latter resented the often uncouth behavior of the lower-class. Although their incomes may have been a contrast, most African-Americans including those of mixed-race, had been relegated to the same section of town. More and more, income differentiated African-American families, but they still had to live among one another.[31]

Physically, the middle-class shows that it is comprised largely of men and women of mixed race.[32] This is the higher income group of the community. While strides were being made on an intragroup basis, there was little impact outside the group. The income of the average African-American family of any given status was always much lower than was the income of the average Euro-American family.[33] The middle-class African-American was better off but not as secure economically as might be thought. The economic foundation for middle-class African-American families was a product of the cooperation of the husband and wife.[34] Certain segments of the population, especially African-American women, did what they could to secure their position on the income ladder. While middle-class African-American women showed a driving preference for mixed-race children, they opposed sexual integration because they feared that African-American men of higher means would no longer have to settle for mixed-race women.[35] Their trade-off to an African-American man of the masses with a high income was their mixed race; Euro-American features gave them an advantage. Thus straight hair, keen noses, and light skin were associated with upper-class status, especially among African-American women.[36]

Mixed-race mulattoes who were from the lower-class moved up with some difficulty. They may have been referred to as "marginals." Marginals might be positioned between subcultures of their own peculiar subculture, as in the case of lower-class mulattoes whose low-class position clashed with high ranking on the racial hierarchy in the African-American subculture. This situation was allowed to occur because the values for race were accepted by all. The American caste order has even more directly stamped the African-American class system by including relative "whiteness" as one of the main factors determining status within the African-American community.[37] By mulatto, and mass African-American standards as well, this is perhaps one of the reasons that the tendency to value mixed race was and is so potent.

V

Fear/Inferiority: Racist
Images of African-American Men

The racial images of Negroid people, i.e., African-Americans, were not always subject to accusations of fear and/or inferiority. Prior to the Atlantic slave trade, race differentiations were first alluded to by ancient Greeks. The Greeks made reference to Negroid skin, however to which classical authors had not yet attached any basic significance. "Ethiopians do not astonish Greeks because of their blackness and their different appearance," wrote Agatharchides.[1] Agatharchides' statement was not only an accurate assessment of the ancient Greek reaction to Negroid skin, but it resonates today as an aspect of childhood known to psychologists. "Four-year-olds," according to Allport, are in fact quite interested, curious, and appreciative of differences in racial groups.[2] Furthermore, Marsh, in considering the awareness of racial differences in African children living in modern day Britain, found that the critical age of racial curiosity seems to be around three to three and a half years.[3] Thus, it would be perfectly normal for a Euro-American child living in a predominantly Western environment to take notice of African-Americans. The reaction of an African child, on first exposure to Caucasian skin, would be similarly innocent and devoid of racism. In documenting his experience in African villages that were previously unexposed to Europeans, the explorer David Livingstone wrote that the moment a child came in contact with Europeans he would "take to his heels in a terror and that the mother, alarmed by the child's wild outcries would rush out of the hut and dart back in again at the first glimpse of the same fearful apparition."[4]

Like Greeks, the ancient Egyptians, whose contacts with Negroid people was seasoned, did not find it necessary to refer to Kushites by race. While Egyptian monarchs of the Twenty-fifth Dynasty, for reasons of artistic stylization, were sometimes painted with dark Negroid skin, neither the lighter skin color of the monarchs nor the darker skin of their subjects was mentioned. The ancient Egyptians had for quite some time been completely at ease with the variations in racial appearance that were apparent among residents of the Nile Valley and thus attached little if any significance to such differences.

In the dawn of Western civilization, documentation of the attitudes toward Africans suggests racism was lacking. Greek references, however, are informative, particularly when they are scrutinized within the context of race. By virtue of historical record, it is possible to examine the early Greek norms for beauty and their implications for Negroid people. The combined Platonic, Lucretian, and Ovidian assumptions of the classical norm image suggest a distaste for extremes. The main characters in classical poetry seem to prefer their own racial attributes to those of the extremely light-skinned Germans or of the dark-skinned Africans.[5] In the aftermath, Greeks, like all people, used themselves as the ideal in their expressions of aesthetic preference. Little mention is made, however, that there were Europeans as well as Africans who did not meet the ideal Greek image.

In some early Western cultures there were those who extolled the beauty of Negroid attributes and did not hesitate to do so publicly. Herodotus, the first known among Westerners to express an opinion about the physical appearance of Africans, described them as the "most handsome of all men."[6] Others, such as Philodemus, put their feelings into poetry. In reference to a certain Philænion, short, black, with hair more curled than parsley and skin tender than down, concludes: "May I love such a Philænion, golden Cypris, until I find another more perfect."[7] Still another, named Asclepiades, praises the beauty of the Negroid Didyme. The poem continues: "Gazing at her beauty I melt like wax before the fire. And if she is black, what difference to me? So are coals when we light them, they shine like rose-buds."[8] Another named Theocritus contends that those who refer to his Bombyca as sunburned should know that to him she is "honey-brown and charming and adds that violets and hyacinths dark but are the first flowers chosen for nosegays."[9]

Citizens of Greek civilization maintained narcissistic norms for racial attributes. In referring to such norms for judging beauty, Harry Hoetink applies the terms "somatic norm image." He defines somatic norm image as "the complex of physical (somatic) characteristics which are accepted by a group as its ideal," pointing out that each group considers itself aesthetically superior to others.[10] To illustrate the somatic norm image, Hoetink makes reference to an African creation myth, in which an African perceives himself as perfectly cooked while a European is underdone due to a defect in the Creator's oven. As a result, Europeans had to be fashioned from clay. The early Greeks would have noted that the physical norms for humanity varied. The Greek Philostratus thus remarked that Indians esteemed "white" less than "black" because, he implied, "black" was the color of Indians.[11] The implications of racial attributes would change radically over time consequent to racism in the modern images of African-American men.

The universal perception of African-American men evolved from the Atlantic slave trade, which necessitated a Western history of racist imagery.[12] Scholars and practitioners amenable to such images permeate the ranks of political, educational, economic, and judicial institutions. Furthermore, those professionals have enabled the validation of imagery in their research and publication of otherwise bogus conclusions that are based on race. Although the literature contains acknowledgement of racist objectives, academia has been less willing to acknowledge those objectives with equal enthusiasm. In the aftermath are images of African-American men as threatening and intellectually dull. In fact they perform poorly—it is assumed via race--on IQ and other standardized test measures of intelligence. These beliefs are relevant to both slavery and the antebellum era.

Images of African-American men have occupied American folklore historically. According to Lippmann, images are "pictures in our heads."[13]

Howard Ehrlich thought of them as "a set of beliefs and dis-beliefs about any group of people."[14] The esteemed Gordon Allport insisted images as "stereotype is an exaggerated belief associated with a category."[15] Much like prejudice, definitions of imagery highlight certain aspects of African-American men while completely ignoring others. Unfortunately, for such men, what is highlighted has been limited to what evokes fear and inferiority.

The Western scientist Lombardo referred to two distinct images, which connoted African-American men.[16] The first is the "brute." The second is "sambo." Both were initially developed by Europeans to secure their position in the current world order and simultaneously denigrate Africans for purposes of inferiorization. The "brute" defined Africans as primitive, temperamental, violent, and sexually powerful, and the "sambo" as child-like hence lacking in intellect. The "brute" in particular was effective in conveying fear of Africans, mental dullness and lack of self-control. Europeans (Caucasians) and their American cohorts then validated race, enabling a status hierarchy between Africans (Negroid) and themselves. Extended from this racist hierarchy is Europeans' racist image of African-American men.

In reality, Euro-Americans have relied on imagery to call attention to racist beliefs that characterize African-American men in a derogatory context. What is more, such images cannot presume the accuracy of fact. Nonetheless, when influenced by racism Euro-Americans apply them to exaggerations or untrue speculations about African-Americans.[17] Even the otherwise intelligent and conscientious person who would reject such racism may firmly believe that the images extend from some element of truth. In fact, a racist image is a communal but unscientifically validated belief about the performances of out-group populations, i.e., people of Negroid descent and particularly African-American men. This assumption acknowledges the existence of in-group images that extend from such beliefs. However, in-group imagery is normally accommodated by the possession of power and are thus favorable images that powerful in-groups ordinarily cherish about themselves.[18] A critical necessity is to expose the groundless and derogatory forms that the powerful Euro-American in-group frequently hold as an extension of Western intellectual superiority. Furthermore, the existence of a derogatory African-American image suggests that those who subscribe to it are at best ignorant or at worst racist. The potency of either is formidable to the extent Euro-Americans fear African-American men who are otherwise law abiding citizens. Thus, racist imagery may influence the behaviors of all races in similar ways that the intellectual images influence the academic performance of African-American students. Subsequently, those who would ascribe to the "dumb" African-American image then attribute any non-Negroid behavior, trait, or talent among African-Americans to luck or European ancestry.

In 1969, psychologist Arthur Jensen published a paper in the *Harvard Educational Review*. It was titled "How Much Can We Boost IQ and Scholastic Achievement?" This paper took the position that government programming for compensatory education had failed. That failure was inherent in an attempt to improve IQ scores particularly as pertains to children of African descent. As is known by psychologists, the IQ scores of African-Americans average less than that of Euro-Americans. Those who disagree with Jensen's position contend that these differences are a result of social and economic disadvantages. As per Jensen, such a rationale justified "wasteful" spending on compensatory educational programs designed to equalize opportunities between citizens of African and European descent. The failure of these programs, according to Jensen, suggests a need to question the presuppositions on which such programs are based, particularly the argument that IQ differences between races are due to environmental influences. Jensen's need to question this argument focus on two major assumptions: 1) IQ tests are valid measurements of intelligence; and 2) methods of estimating the racial component of IQ are valid. Succinctly put, the racial component of IQ is the extent to which IQ differences between persons of

African (Negroid) and European (Caucasian) descent are due to genetic heritage, i.e., race. Absent rigorous scientific methodology, Jensen proposes that environment accounts for only about 20% of the IQ differences between such groups.[19]

The crux of Jensen's argument is shared by other psychologists, such as Richard Herrnstein, who prefers to stress class differences as the rationale. According to Herrnstein's research, upper- and middle-class children score significantly superior to working class children. Jensen does not refute Herrnstein's class differences because both ultimately agree on the race rationale. Thus, in 1995, Herrnstein teamed with Charles Murray—a political scientist--and published the controversial *The Bell Curve*.[20] *The Bell Curve* is a voluminous study about the assumed inherited intelligence differential between persons of African and European descent. According to the authors, race will dictate socioeconomic achievement, social pathology, and intelligence, which will be increasingly unequally distributed across the world's racial populations. As societies become more technological they contend that stratification by cognitive ability will prevail. Given the racial nature of this phenomenon social programs and other government compensatory interventions are then ineffective and a waste of tax dollars. This notion is the grist of imagery that has permeated academy since the antebellum. Accordingly, *The Bell Curve* is heretofore unsubstantiated as a valid premise that manages some validity extended from the prestige of modern science on which media images of African-American men are based, i.e., "Stepin Fetchit."

According to Bogle, print media said the following about African-American stereotype Stepin Fetchit: "[He] has been missing appointments for 32 years ... is the world's champion job-loser. Because of his intolerable memory, he has been thrown out of all the best American race meetings, lost several distinguished positions as a shoe-black and forfeited one of the biggest starring contracts Hollywood had to offer--they could never find him."[21] Stepin Fetchit was simultaneously Hollywood's ultimate inferior. He more than any other African-American male represented to Euro-American audiences an image they controlled.

Stepin Fetchit was born in 1902, in Key West, Florida, as Lincoln Theodore Monroe Andrew Perry, and was named after four presidents. He arrived in Hollywood during the late 1920s. His original aspiration was--according to media--to become a preacher. However, he got involved with acting instead. His name extends from a comic act he worked called "Step and Fetch It."[22] A talent scout saw him, invited him for a screen test, and the rest is history.

By the age of thirty-two, Stepin Fetchit was the African-American, stereotypical darling of Hollywood. America was unprepared for the emergence of this intellectually slow, dim-witted film actor. Even fewer could have predicted the impact he would have on an entire era. Nevertheless, Stepin Fetchit succeeded far beyond what would have been expected of an African-American man in the 1930s because his talent served Euro-American audiences psychologically. Ironically, he was the most successful and well known African-American actor of his time. In a span of six years he appeared in twenty-six films made by Fox Pictures. It was not unusual for him to work in as many as four movies at a time. Astonishingly, Stepin Fetchit was the first African-American successful enough to merit featured billing, something normally reserved for Euro-Americans. In addition, in an effort to appeal to Euro-American audiences, special scenes would be written to include him. The Euro-American public was fascinated with this African-American clown who had taken his stammer and shoe shuffling to new heights. In fact, so convincing was Fetchit in the role he played that audiences believed he actually could not run. His fame and notoriety were said to influence even the walk and demeanor of young African-American males on the streets.[23]

The film industry took advantage of every opportunity to exploit the images Fetchit so successful conveyed. They circulated rumors about his private affairs, which included a flamboyant lifestyle, six houses, sixteen Chinese servants, two-thousand-dollar cashmere suits imported from India, lavish parties, and twelve cars.[24] His image as a clown included ownership of a champagne-pink Cadillac complete with his name in neon lights. Audiences who read of Fetchit's private life were even more drawn to his films because he seemed to fit in real life what they saw of him on screen.

Perhaps to his credit, Fetchit was a little more astute than the images he portrayed in film. On some level he became aware of the Euro-American fascination with "...those lazy, no-account, good-for-nothin-forever-in-hot-water" African-Americans at whom Euro-Americans loved to laugh. Here was the ultimate inferior dim-wit who served to calm Euro-American fears of African-American aggression. In acting the image of a clown Fetchit became what Bogle referred to as the "arch-coon" of Hollywood.[25] He had no equal in the stammering, shuffling, dim-witted schemes from which later clowns would draw. His name and demeanor were perfect for the part. He was rail thin, tall, and noted for being completely bald. His clothes also fit the part as they were often too large, giving the impression they had been passed down from "de ol massa." To complete the image, Fetchit played to the camera with a wide grin, visible white teeth, and head bowed. He walked very slow as if in need of a map to wherever he might be going. His speech was slow as well, emphasizing his poor English and obviously dull-wit. Fetchit was either a genius in portraying this image or simply a well paid African-American man who actually was a clown. Nevertheless, Euro-American audiences found him convincing enough to support his success. One critic wrote after seeing him dance in a movie, "Mr. Fetchit's feet are like chained lightning as he performs."[26] Thus, the worth of his inferiority was so valued and so effective as to evoke comedy even in criticism.

In every media image, the well-rounded African-American man was conspicuously absent.[27] Except for *Birth of a Nation*, which extolled fear by the usual rape fantasies, acceptable images limited roles for African-American men to the passive clown and buffoon.[28] Stepin Fetchit was unprecedented, and symbolized the ideal embodiment of antebellum "white supremacy."[29] This dull-witted, slow-moving, wide-eyed character was embraced throughout the country as preferred African-American male prototype in response to Birth of a Nation. Stepin Fetchit's foot shuffling and head scratching evoked pitiful laughter from the audience. He was, for all intents and purposes, non-threatening and sexless--the essence needed to calm Euro-American fear. His character was eventually laid to rest by the African-American community's protest.

The ultimate function of the African-American clown is an historical image to rationalize lack of intelligence. In a 1943 survey conducted with Euro-American school children by Blake and Dennis, it was determined that the most popular image of African-Americans was the assumption of their overall low intelligence.[30] They were characterized by such traits as ignorance and servitude. What is more, in Katz and Braly's study at Princeton University, African-Americans were described by the most negative adjectives, many of which reflected on their general inability to think. That inability was further exploited by Hollywood in the clown images of Amos 'n Andy.

Following the heyday of Stepin Fetchit, Amos n' Andy were perhaps the characters of radio, film, and television who were most loved by Euro-Americans.[31] The two primary characters embodied the clown effectively. Kingfish, the clown, was constantly applying his obviously dull-wit to concoct schemes for extracting money from Amos and Andy. In an equally inferior role, Amos and Andy were constantly taken in, long after the audience had caught on, until the last minute when a confrontation would ensue. A nagging, complaining African-American woman, named Sapphire, was occasionally brought in to mediate. Night after night, audiences were entertained by disputes between the characters. They were popular because they were non-threatening; they were the psychological antidotes to the threatening African-American images that necessarily remained suppressed.

Following World War II, television replaced radio in popularity. Its moving pictures brought images to life in a way that print or radio could not. More than any other component of modern media, television is by far the most potent for stereotypes. Since the advent of cable TV, virtually every home across America has access to its programming. More so than print and radio, television is intimate. Its ability to drive home the stereotype of the African-American male was politically exploited, during a presidential election year, in the person of Willie Horton.[32] There was nothing new about this old image, but television allowed viewers to "pseudoexperience" Mr. Horton. It was assumed that citizens, both male and female, would then go out and vote accordingly. At any rate, George H. W. Bush, whose election team had exploited the image, did in fact win the 1988 presidential campaign.[33]

No less given to the contrived images of African-American men, modern print media is formidable as a means of communicating fear and inferiority. What people cannot learn verbally they can read or have the literate read to them. Although print was not new compared to screen images early on, it was largely an unregulated industry.[34] Individual attempts by companies within the industry to put ethics before profit might very well have led to bankruptcy; this reality prompted some tabloids to exploit African-American violence by reporting in a manner that was sure to incite, merely for the purpose of increasing sales.[35] One of the most brutal events in recent history occurred in New York City.

Late one evening, an upper-middle-class investment broker was taking her daily jog through the ill-famed Central Park. Known as the "Central Park Jogger," the victim was violently attacked and raped.[36] It was an old antebellum theme: African-American men and fear. The print media incited a frenzy around the case by describing the accused African-Americans as "animals" and a "pack." They became the featured story of tabloids around the country for a number of successive weeks. In this circus-like atmosphere, judicial prudence may have been compromised. It was as if guilt bad been assumed, and the presumption of "innocent until proven guilty" did not apply in such cases.

To further exploit racist images of African-American men, the print media will employ visual aides.[37] In the 19th century, pre-photography era this was accomplished via cartoons. The most menacing style possible was used to portray African-American men, in a way that would justify the assumption being peddled.[38] If the assumption was intellectual inferiority, his lips and feet were drawn in a comic, protruding manner that would evoke laughter. If the assumptions were fear, the skin was necessarily dark, the figure imposing, and the face, if shown, revealing an angry lust. Few words were ever needed to communicate the message of such cartoons; they were already ingrained in the American psyche and easily exploitable by those who controlled the media.[39]

Effective as print was in portraying images of African-American men via cartoons and other drawings, the potential impact of racism was increased with the invention of photography; following the invention of the camera, the African-American image could be displayed in greater detail. The photograph had the ability to freeze a detailed likeness of a person who could then be recognized on sight. The print media --motivated by profit-- learned to use lighting, pose, attire, etc., to create images of the aggressive offender; this continues even today. The alleged defendants in the case of the Central Park Jogger were photographed in dark glasses with solemn expressions on their faces, as if to make their guilt all the more believable.[40] Hence, Euro-Americans with a motive accuse African-American men of violent crimes that they themselves commit.

In a 1990 Boston, Massachusetts, crime an African-American was accused of murdering a pregnant, Euro-American housewife, Mrs. Stuart. The entire nation assumed the guilt of the accused, an African-American man named Bennett, based on media hype and its larger than life photographs of the murder scene. Only after one of the accomplices involved in the frame-up came forth to reveal the truth, that the husband was the murderer, was Bennett released from police custody.[41] The belief that Bennett was guilty as charged was arguably, in large part, a reaction to his race.

A more recent and dramatic manifestation of the African-American male criminal stereotype perpetrated by mass media is the case of Susan Smith. According to Mrs. Smith, convicted of murdering her two children, she had been attacked by an African-American male; in the aftermath, she said the unknown assailant had drowned her young sons and escaped with her car. Well aware of the criminal stereotype, Smith assumed that the all too believable scenario of the criminal would go unquestioned in the Southern town of Union, South Carolina. Fortunately, police were not so reluctant to question the case. Their investigation led to the arrest and conviction of Smith, the accuser. Lost in the account of what had occurred was the fact that a African-American male had been cited as culprit in the crime. Mass media's major headlines emphasized the drowning of two children while ignoring the criminal indictment of an entire group of innocent citizens.[42] In addition, in perhaps the trial of the century, a darkened photo of O.J. Simpson appeared on the cover of *Time* magazine as an even more dramatic illustration of distorted media imagery. While it is debatable why the media portrays such, what cannot be disputed is the fact that too many dark-skinned Americans are characterized, regardless of demography, by stress-inducing images.[43]

The implication of racist imagery reinforces the perception of African-American men as hostile and aggressive, which is a fairly common notion as pertains to much of the existing research.[44] One study conducted by Devine was able to illustrate that regardless of whether or not the subject is known to be prejudiced, most Euro-Americans think of African-Americans as aggressive and/or dull-witted.[45] For this and other reasons, the American public has been unwilling to accept African-American men in television roles where they are too intelligent, or otherwise too polite, in an effort to rescue Euro-American self-concept. More recently, Avery Brooks starred in a television series entitled *A Man*

Called Hawk, which was a spin-off of another series called *Spenser For Hire*. His role was perhaps the most ambitious for a Black man that has been attempted to date. In the series, a masculine African-American man with a shaved head and facial hair roamed Washington, D.C., fighting crime. He drove a black BMW and carried a very large chrome-plated magnum hand gun. While he sought to uphold the law, he was not a law enforcement officer. He did not act freely and independently, but at the directives of his Euro-American counterpart, Spenser. The original character of Hawk was non-threatening because the role implied that he was being controlled. While *Spencer for Hire*, with the original Hawk character, was not a big hit, it was far more successful than *A Man Called Hawk*.[46]

Davis has unveiled a motive for the African-American image as a racist preoccupation emanating from fear generated within the Euro-American status quo.[47] He presumes that members of the group anticipate losing economic, political, and educational control. In the aftermath is a motive for investigating the so-called inferiority of African-American men and their IQ deficiency. In the past, they were assumed to be deficient and denied access to competition with Euro-Americans for two reasons: (1) the country practiced segregation; and (2) it was believed that Euro-Americans were superior. Once society became integrated and Americans of African descent began to succeed, Euro-Americans rationalized that it was due to unfair government policies. This notion assured the image of Caucasian superiority and Negroid inferiority for competition in corporate boardrooms and political arenas. In the aftermath, a Euro-American status quo was assumed to be secure.

The trepidation and apprehension of Euro-Americans cause them to necessarily subjugate African-American men by race—including science and media--to maintain a caste system of privilege and opportunity that has operated for decades.[48] When African-Americans perform at their optimal capacity in an environment unpolluted by racist imagery, humankind will benefit. At the turn of a century it is indeed appropriate to put to rest pseudo-scientific myths that have prevailed on the efforts of many irrespective of race, creed, color, and/or gender.

VI

Affirmative Action: The Racial Divide

Race, among the five categories of discriminatory attributes and as written into affirmative action legislation, unfairly eliminates whole groups within the population from equal employment and education opportunities.[1] For this reason, affirmative action was enacted but has become the racial divide and counterproductive, which politically--and thus legally—has limited its application. Today it is on the verge of being completely eliminated despite its overall benefit to general society. Those who oppose it are not overtly racists, as would be characteristic of eugenicists or "white supremacists," but their stealth is more formidable given the facade of fairness. Intended or not, the racism served by those who oppose affirmative action is a continuation of past policies.

Racism remains among America's most tenacious and heated of social problems. Its mere mention provokes such intense feelings that Euro-Americans, in particular those who oppose affirmative action, avoid commenting during polite conversations. African-Americans conversely are more amenable because they understand that any efforts to eliminate racism will require institutional and/or policy changes. Being more amenable to challenging racism in jobs and college admissions, African-Americans willingly confront the fact that aside from being a social problem racism functions as an historical tradition of Euro-Americans to exclude African-Americans and other minority groups from sharing in the wealth of opportunities being an American citizen can offer.[2] In this sense racism is different from other societal nemesis in that it is sustained not only by bigots but otherwise civil minded law abiding citizens whose motives are not tainted by malice. When pressed to discussion they abhor racism, knowing full well that having to live life as an African-American would destine them to a lesser share of available opportunities having committed no criminal acts. For it is the color of Negroid skin, which identifies race and serves as a means by which African-Americans, and other non-Caucasians, are excluded. Likewise, those who are identified by skin color as Caucasian have been historically afforded the best opportunities for education, employment and other quality of life possibilities.[3] It is such historical advantages vis-à-vis race that the proponents of Affirmative Action have attempted to address.

Within the context of civil rights and equal opportunity: "All personnel actions affecting employees or applicants for employment shall be made free from any discrimination based on race, color, religion, sex, or national origin."[4] This language is the essence of affirmative action laws. While no one can argue the moral worth of racial discrimination laws like Affirmative Action, response to the application of such laws has been much less noble.

Civil minded Americans who oppose affirmative action have regarded it as an unfair labor law imposed on them by the federal government. Most are ignorant about the origin of such a complex issue. In 1996, my paper tracing the concept of affirmative action to the 1930s appeared in the *Journal of Sociology and Social Welfare*.[5] What it reveals would refute the accusation of Euro-Americans who insist affirmative action is unfair and punishes those who happen to be Caucasian for acts they had nothing to do with: a kind of "reverse discrimination." The United States *Congressional Record* of 1935 gives an official account of affirmative action's earlier purpose. It did not originate during the Kennedy and Johnson administrations, but, in fact, much sooner. According to *Record*, the concept of affirmative action was originally applied in 1935 for the benefit of Euro-American males "preferably of non-Jewish stock." They were fighting powerful industrialists of the time in attempting to organize themselves into a union. Critics of the day did not attack it as "preferential treatment" or "reverse discrimination." All recognized the value to society that would come as the result of its enactment.[6]

Having served Euro-American interests, affirmative action lay dormant for several decades. In an effort to combat racism, which most Americans will admit is a factor, activists revisited it in the 1960s to enable non-Caucasian-Americans to compete for jobs and education on level ground with more privileged Euro-Americans. At some point Euro-Americans became disillusioned by the complaints of friends and family members who insisted they could not get admitted to college or find employment because a "less qualified" minority—an African-American--was chosen. Their anger and frustration festered until the election of Ronald Reagan to the presidency in 1980. He, more than any other, spoke to their concerns giving permission to the mainstream as well as the bigot to revert to past attitudes when employment advantages of Euro-Americans based on their racial identity was the norm.

Thus, affirmative action may be passively enforced today by conservative political administrations and may be in jeopardy of complete elimination. Those opposed to it insist that affirmative action violates equal protection under the law and sets up a process popularized by the Bakke decision as "reverse discrimination." Consequently, affirmative action became arguably the most heated issue attacked by conservatives, such as Utah Senator Orrin Hatch. It is his contention that mere debate about affirmative action cannot occur without the perception of malice on the part of proponents. Not to be taken in by Hatch's motive, proponents believe Senator Hatch and his cohorts intend to dismantle affirmative action without proposing any alternative for correcting the past injustices, which all agree prevails. While true to some extent, Euro-Americans like Hatch ignore the complex web of race traditions--such as those pertaining to college admissions and employment--that are not only irrelevant to the acts of "innocent" Euro-Americans, but benefit them nonetheless.[7] Thus, aside from racists, Euro-Americans in opposition to affirmative action have little or no knowledge of history in suggesting it is unfair.

Post-WWII efforts to equalize opportunity across racial groups were initiated in opposition to labor practices by the Labor Department. In the 1960s, the Labor Department's Office of Federal Contract Compliance (OFCC) became the target of activists whose objective was to remove obstacles to equal employment opportunities for African-Americans—especially as pertains to union membership. By 1967, activists had moved the OFCC to require a written quota schedule or otherwise take "affirmative action" in eliminating the problem. Building trades and the unions who operate with them were faced with providing employment opportunities for African-Americans, which they had denied in the past based on racial discrimination. At some point the OFCC adopted an action-oriented policy providing contracts solely to businesses that set specific targets for employing African-American and other race minorities. Their policy was referred to as the Philadelphia Plan. Endorsed by President Johnson, the OFCC tested the numerical "timetable" plan in St. Louis, Cleveland, and Philadelphia.[8]

While most conservative opponents of affirmative action attribute quotas to Democrats like Kennedy and Johnson, fact does not support their assumptions. "It was the Nixonites who gave us employment quotas.[9] In fact few scholars have been willing to assign credit to Republicans for affirmative action law perhaps for the same reason few can comment accurately on its origin. In fact it was the Republican Richard Nixon, of Watergate fame, who initially approved specific goals and timetables to eliminate obstacles to African-American employment and college admissions. What is more, at some point Nixon had been considered by civil rights activists, such as James Farmer, "as the most adamant among presidents in support of Affirmative Action."[10] No doubt scholars are not united regarding the level of his support and/or involvement. According to *Presidential Studies Quarterly,* Hood attributed Nixon's support of affirmative action to his personal belief that racial equality must become fact. Others, such as Hoff, concurred, pointing out Nixon's longstanding support of African-Americans that dated back to his role as Vice President during the Eisenhower administration.[11]

Those who are more suspicious, such as Graham, refer to Nixon's political ambitions, his complex personality, his ambiguity about civil rights, and otherwise random approach to policy. Furthermore, Graham notes Nixon's desertion of affirmative action as he approached the 1972 election campaign. While most scholars tend to give Nixon some credit for Affirmative Action, they consider his support staff as being more responsible in bringing it about.[12]

Whether one is inclined to give Nixon credit for affirmative action, his personality was a contributing factor to this confusion. He was known to be difficult to predict in his cynicism, manipulation, idealism, and courage. The way he approached domestic policy and the hiring and firing of staff reflected that complexity. By this some would suggest that Nixon's opposition to racial discrimination and his political objectives were among the motives that impacted his approach to affirmative action. Considering his personal views and political risks, Nixon could be a staunch supporter of affirmative action and at times completely aloof. While Vice President, he was adamant about eliminating racial discrimination in employment practices. Once he became President, Nixon then approved of the "Philadelphia Plan" devised under the earlier Kennedy and Johnson administrations. However, when such a plan presented an obstacle to his support by Euro-American blue-collar workers, he disowned it. Due to his personality and unpredictable support, affirmative action then developed into a complex network of applications instituted by departmental bureaucrats who realized sporadic degrees of success.[13] Hence, in practice, affirmative action did not develop according to any single formula or design. Instead, it evolved slowly and randomly as the federal government acted to integrate Euro-American construction unions to include African-Americans.

The application of affirmative action to the building trade unions was a politically intense undertaking. To maintain Euro-American advantage and a high wage structure, unions historically limited membership by denying African-Americans admission to their apprenticeship programs. Only Euro-American friends or family members could be admitted to such programs and, ultimately, the union. Ironically, the rhetoric of the AFL-CIO voiced strong support of equal opportunity and the Civil Rights Act of 1964. In practice, at least in the building trades, most denied membership to African-Americans based solely on race. "When I was a plumber, AFL-CIO President George Meany once remarked, it never occurred to me to have niggers in the union."[14] Thus, by 1967, African-Americans constituted a mere eight percent of construction trade union membership, the plumbing workers, sheet-metal, electrical, asbestos, and elevator operators for a total of only 1,400 out of a membership of 330,000.[15]

Prior to the Nixon and Kennedy administrations, the federal government all but ignored racial discrimination in the trade unions. To eliminate it in businesses associated with the federal government, in 1953, President Eisenhower organized the President's Committee on Government Contracts. Its chairmen was the then Vice President, Richard Nixon. However, the committee was more hype than effect, due to it having been restricted in what it could do. Aware of Congressional attitude and the opposition of Southern politicians, Eisenhower ordered committee members to press for "justice and equality through leadership and persuasion" because coercion and punishment might offend Southern interests. Above all, Eisenhower did not want the committee to be seen as a federal "Fair Employment Practices Commission" that would have the authority to investigate racial discrimination and impose penalties. Eisenhower feared that such a commission would incite unwanted racial disturbances on the part of Euro-Americans.[16] In response to Eisenhower's orders, Nixon addressed complaints of racial discrimination by separate cases and attempted to persuade those employers in violation to alter any racist hiring practices. As a result, Nixon's committee was obviously against any quotas or timetables. It is also on record as never having canceled a contract or boycotted any employer found in violation.[17]

Due to governmental passivity most labor unions ignored the request to open their apprenticeship programs to African-Americans. Without any enforcement efforts among other issues, the President's Committee on Government Contracts was unable to eliminate racial discrimination in the hiring of African-Americans for skilled jobs. AFL-CIO officials attempted to convey progress by citing statistics showing increases in African-American union membership. Additionally, George Meany, a member of the committee, rescued unions in his refusal to compel union officials to admit more African-Americans. As a trade-off for the AFL-CIO's promotion of non-Communist labor unions abroad, Nixon would not advocate for increased African-American membership. In a rare exception during 1960, the committee did obtain employment for three African-Americans on a federal construction project in Washington, D.C. Immediately, the NAACP charged that at such a pace it would take African-Americans 138 years to acquire equal access with Euro-Americans to the building trades.[18]

In opposing racial discrimination in the building trades, former Presidents Kennedy and Johnson were much more deliberate than their Republican predecessor, Eisenhower. In 1963, African-Americans risked considerable police violence to picket Philadelphia's building trade unions, which were for the most part directed by Euro-American interests. In response to rioting, President Kennedy ordered the Committee on Equal Employment Opportunity to oversee the employment practices of those who sought construction contracts from the federal government. After Kennedy was assassinated, Johnson carried forward by signing Executive Order 1124, which re-established the federal government's support of "equal employment opportunity" for those companies holding contracts or intending to do business with the federal government. Both Kennedy and Johnson supported affirmative action, but did not themselves propose specific goals or timetables for building trade and construction unions to follow.[19]

The 1964 Civil Rights act was a failed attempt to redress racial discrimination. In an effort to circumvent that failure, affirmative action was one of a number of policies that facilitated the admission of more African-Americans to college and hiring in professions otherwise historically denied to them on the basis of race.[20] Today, affirmative action may be passively enforced by conservative political administrations and may be in jeopardy of complete elimination.[21] Critics contend that it violates equal protection under the law and sets up a process of "reverse discrimination."[22] They further suggest that affirmative action will benefit minorities who are not victims of racial discrimination and, because of hiring practices, will punish Euro-Americans who are "innocent" of any wrongdoing. Such assumptions are naive and reflect the spoils of power. While true to some extent, the same critics ignore the complex web of racial issues met by minorities that are not only irrelevant to the deliberate acts of "innocent" Euro-Americans, but in many cases create an advantage.[23] A culture that enables advantage on the basis of race cannot exist without creating opportunity bias and a racial hierarchy.

The legal and political assault on affirmative action efforts make it difficult to establish equal opportunity and eliminate racial discrimination. The state of Texas has suspended several minority scholarship programs for minority race students. Its law school has been barred from using racial preferences for admissions and awarding financial aid to needy African- and Latino-Americans. In California, a three judge panel of the U.S. Court of Appeals for the Fifth Circuit undercut the California State Supreme Court's decision regarding the 1978 Bakke case by finding affirmative action programs to be illegal.[24] Critics insist their efforts are not intended to hurt minorities, but to see to it that Euro-Americans are not discriminated against in the process.

Aside from faculty hires and student admissions the attacks on affirmative action include an array of educational decisions brought by legal action. At the University of North Carolina, a law student claiming "reverse discrimination" contended his civil rights had been violated. Of the 32 member university board, 4 seats have been reserved for minorities and women. As a Euro-American male, the student contended that his right to equal protection under the Fourteenth

Amendment of the U.S. Constitution were being trampled.[25] The failure of affirmative action in each case can be attributed to it having been poorly worded. In an attempt to eliminate discrimination it does in fact discriminate--particularly, against Euro-American males. That should not suggest, however, that affirmative action has no merit. Instead, it must be re-written on the basis of a criterion that is more quantifiable and less subject to personal interpretation. Euro-American advantage has long been an overlooked basis of racial discrimination and is vehicle to the disproportionate numbers of those in college and the most lucrative professions.[26]

The Bakke case is most critical to affirmative action in recent times. This case involved a thirty-five-year-old Euro-American man who had applied more than once for admission to the University of California Medical School at Davis. He was denied each time. Angered by what he thought of as preferential treatment of African-Americans, Bakke criticized the school's policies. For each entering class of 100 students, sixteen places were reserved for "qualified" minorities in adherence to the University's Affirmative Action Program. The school clearly acknowledged the historical racism of unfair exclusions from the medical profession that African-Americans and other minorities had encountered. Bakke's test scores were reported to exceed those of minority students who had been allowed one of the sixteen reserved places. As if test scores correlated to merit based admission, he complained about this first to the local California courts, then ultimately to the U. S. Supreme Court. He insisted that his inability to be admitted to medical school was based solely on his race.[27]

According to Bakke, the University of California violated his Fourteenth Amendment right to equal protection under the law and the Civil Rights Act of 1964. His claims were attributed to the school practicing an affirmative action policy that resulted in his being rejected without cause. The case was a bit complex in that, dependent on one's political view, an equally valid argument could be made for or against. Those involved had no single majority opinion. A number of Justices who heard the case contended that any racial quota system set up by the federal government violated the Civil Rights Act of 1964. In support, Justice Lewis F. Powell, Jr., agreed and cast the deciding vote, which required the medical school to admit Bakke. Powell, however, went further in his opinion stating that the rigid use of racial quotas applied by the school had violated the equal protection clause of the Fourteenth Amendment. His cohorts added that the use of race as a factor in admission decisions to medical school and other institutions of higher education were allowed by the Constitution. All Justices found that the application of race was possible when considered among other admission criteria. Thus, the Justices were able to quiet Euro-American opposition to affirmative action while at the same time retaining the gains made by African-American and other minorities over the years.[28]

For minorities, the issue of race continues to negatively influence employees and/or applicants seeking admission to college and employment at predominantly Euro-American institutions.[29] Concern for its influence is frequently subordinated in lieu of so-called "fairness." Furthermore, a society that values workers for their racial attributes necessitates that race, if implied by color, influence occupational opportunity through the limitations of aspiration.[30] The objective of affirmative action was to offer an alternative that could be used for the betterment of society. Unfortunately, many such efforts have been denigrated by individual Euro-Americans whose marginal qualifications have not enabled their goals. By exploring the impact of race on the ability of a selected population of African-Americans, it is obvious that some institutional measure should be the basis of compensating for past injustices. Laws and policies written more accurately may eliminate accusations of "reverse discrimination" and provide a doable method for the establishment of justice and equality on which the sovereignty was founded.

In the shadows of affirmative action, the most bigoted of Euro-Americans believe they are superior to African-Americans as a matter of biological fact.

They have been raised to think that, based on race, they have been endowed with a greater intellectual capacity. Thus, by their value-laden definition of merit they assume themselves to be more deserving than others, who are not Caucasian, of the best educational and employment opportunities the nation has to offer. They see no relevance in the obvious advantages of their being Caucasian and the willingness of society to accommodate their success. While lynching and voting rights issues are a thing of the past, current debates around college admissions and employment policies are little more than a thinly veiled racist mindset. The ultimate aim is the dismantling of past attempts to level the playing field for African-American and other minorities who have been disadvantaged by years of racial discrimination. By dismantling affirmative action on the basis that it is unfair, Euro-Americans are able to circumvent accusations that it is racist and simultaneously enable the opportunity status quo. In doing so, they have encouraged the institutionalization of what Euro-American professor McIntosh refers to as "white privilege."[31]

Regarding "white privilege," Euro-Americans may say they are against racism when what they really mean is they are against the individual kinds of racism. They refuse to recognize that as a group they benefit from institutional and systemic racism against African-Americans and other minorities. Thus, all Euro-Americans are the beneficiaries of a racist system that bestows on them inherited advantage. For them to admit otherwise would render it impossible to deny shared responsibility in the exploitation of African- and other non-Euro-Americans.

Regarding the confines of daily life, Euro-Americans as a group appear less than willing to address the existence of "white privilege" while at the same time granting that African-Americans and other minorities are acutely disadvantaged. The less bigoted profess efforts for equal rights that encompass society's most prestigious and powerful institutions, stopping short of any effort that would limit "white privilege." Such efforts buffer the privileges of said Americans from legitimate discussion because ultimately they have power.

In a non-Totalitarian society, certain disparities in power impact its institutions. The framers of the U.S. Constitution took careful steps to ensure American power remained the possession of Caucasian race groups. Initially, only Europeans and other such groups could immigrate and settle in the U.S. This is a passive form of discrimination acted out against Negroids and Mongoloids by those in the power-race group. It is also the historical genesis of a racial divide in America that precipitates an "us" against "them" mentality whereby African-American and other non-Caucasians may be perceived by Euro-Americans as an alien outgroup. This notion of an "us" against "them" racial divide may be a contributing factor to current accusations that affirmative action is unfair and discriminates against "innocent" Euro-Americans. As a result, mere discussion has been all but civil due to the fact that power is distributed by race and those in power do not perceive affirmative action as beneficial to them personally. Thus, when educational institutions, such as the University of Michigan, along with major business interests allude to the benefits of affirmative action for society, findings are, at best, tacitly received by Euro-Americans.

Unfortunately, assessing affirmative action in the context of power sounds aggressive, and otherwise like an unfair strategy of racists. In an effort to appear fair Euro-Americans couch their opposition to affirmative action in the context of fairness despite historical contradiction. Without commenting directly, understood by all is the fact that power extends to those in authority. Any national policy or law must then serve those in authority by virtue of having power.[32] At the core of affirmative action is an attempt to empower non-Caucasian racial groups that they might compete equally with their Euro-American counterparts for education and employment opportunities. Succinctly put is the redistribution of power in the empowerment of minority race groups.

Jones would imply that an empowered person has pride and is confident in his or her ability to act, and this belief will sustain capable action.[33] A challenge for the Euro-American community in its conviction to be fair is to determine what is most valued in the conduct of American policies. Simply voicing the rhetoric of fairness and abhorring racism without specific calls to action are pointless.

In a power driven society that values citizens for their amount of capital, having power can determine quality of life and opportunity. The intent of affirmative action recognized the need to empower African-Americans so that it might bring about the necessary changes for a more civil and conducive democracy. Affirmative action was considered a solution that was influenced by the political events of recent decades.[34] Among those that were historically prominent are various movements beginning with the Chicago Settlement House;[35] the most recent is the 1964 Civil Rights movement. For those Euro-Americans who supported this legislation in the main, empowerment of minorities and women was not irrelevant to the empowerment of society at-large. However, concern for society at-large is frequently subordinated in lieu of "political correctness," blurring the lines between what is fair and what may extend from differentiations in power.

Ultimately to live in a democratic society one must adhere to a balance between personal rights and rights of others. Certainly the efforts on the part of American ideals is a legacy devoted to that objective. However, the implications of race and power induced by the capricious fulfillment of democratic ideals will wear at the moral fiber of a true democracy. In order to circumvent chaos, a way must be found whereby affirmative action and similar policies can be valued far above personal rights and/or gains. If this does not happen, the distortion will preclude a true democracy. In such an environment the philosophical traditions of the sovereignty and the democracy under which it operates cannot be sustained.

VII

The Politics of Race

Most Americans would be surprised to know the origin of the Republican Party, given that the Democratic Party was founded several years before the Republican Party.[1] The current racism associated with conservative Republicans is a source or irony as well, considering their initial issues. Among the noted issues are included strong opposition to slavery, passing of the Civil Rights Act of 1866 (recognizing African-Americans as citizens), and the Voting Rights Act, which guaranteed participation in elections regardless of race, creed, or previous servitude. In fact, it was the Republican Party that ended slavery with Lincoln's "Emancipation Proclamation". What is more, it was the leadership of the same party that emphasized free speech and women's rights.[2] Those who were against slavery could not find a voice in the dominant, more racist Democratic or Whig parties, which led to the founding of Republicans. The Whig party did not last very long and the Democratic party splintered over the slave race issue, all which made the Republican Party a viable alternative and, thus, formidable opponent.[3]

In 1860, the Republican candidate for President, Abraham Lincoln, won a majority of the electoral votes with a decisive victory. However, that victory was owed to various sections of the country. The only states that supported Lincoln were California and Oregon, where concerns about slavery were the deciding factor. Hence, the Republican Party was the first and only third party to solidify the two-party system. Its victory did not fare well with antagonistic Southern states, which chose to secede rather than give up their rights to own slaves. In total there were 11 such states which gave the Republicans complete control of the federal government. That control and the secession of Southern states led to the Civil War. Soon thereafter the Republicans would be known for their stance on race and Civil Rights and rescue of the downtrodden, but not for long.[4]

It is the contention of some historians that Republicans supported civil rights and the abolition of slavery as a strategy for gaining control of the White House. Whether or not this is true, support of civil rights and the slavery issue were extremely sensitive topics for discussion and could easily have destroyed the careers of aspiring politicians. Given the obvious loyalty of Republicans to issues significant to African-Americans, African-Americans first entered Congress, in 1869, as members of the Republican Party.[5] It was not until 1935 that an African-American would be elected to Congress as a Democrat.

Democrats are among the oldest of traditional political parties in the U.S. Their beginnings extend from a coalition formed by Thomas Jefferson during the 1790s. The objective was to resist the policies of George Washington's administration. Ironically, this coalition referred to itself as Republican, but later changed its name to the Democratic-Republican Party. That coalition eventually separated into the Whig Party with the remaining members making up what is today known as the Democratic Party.[6]

Much of what modern day Republicans espouse were in fact originally Democratic ideals. Such issues as national security were of great importance. Regarding economic and social policy, Democrats emphasized minimum or no government involvement. In effect, they thought the U.S. government should do nothing that the state and other localities could do for themselves. The racial issues of civil rights and slavery were all but non-existent. Thus, few African-Americans, if any were supporters of the early Democratic Party. Euro-Americans who did support the party were primarily Southern plantation owners and immigrant workers located in Northern cities. Both maintained a vehement disdain for the involvement of the federal government in local affairs. Their Republican contemporary, on the other hand, sought the use of government to promote, regulate, correct, and reform whenever and wherever necessary—a likely resentment of Reconstruction.[7]

Democrats, in their emphasis on individual rights, won many local and state elections after 1860. They were especially successful in taking advantage of the race issue in Northern states, where there was Euro-American hostility toward African-Americans. Simultaneously, the South became a formidable voting bloc. Unfortunately none of this was enough to bring in substantial numbers of new voters or convince Republicans to switch parties for purposes of gaining national power immediately following the Civil War. Until the Great Depression, those who were members of the Democratic Party were in the minority vis-a-vis national politics.[8] The few successes came as a result of dissention within the Republican fold.

By the beginning of the 20th century, Democrats remained defined nationally by their minority status among voters. Once again a Republican split helped elect a president, however Democrats were not served due to America's involvement in WWI. Many German- and Irish-Americans were dismayed by the nation's having sided with England. Again the Republicans benefited with a landslide political victory in 1920. For the remainder of the decade the Democrats were disabled by factionalism. The dissention was between urban-ethnic groups and the traditionally racist South. By 1928, Irish Catholic Al Smith compromised a united South, part of which converted to the Republican side for arguably racial reasons.[9]

By middle of the 20th century, the reputation of the Democratic Party began to change. African-Americans had remained Republican up to that point. The so-called New Deal would do much to encourage a majority of those who were registered Republicans to become Democrats. The Democrats were evolving, becoming less dominated by the racist South and more open to government intervention via the economy and various social issues. Furthermore, Democrats were now willing to regulate and assist in the redistribution of wealth, which they had previously opposed. African-Americans whom they considered less of an issue now loomed large as they sought to assist those least able in a more complex, sophisticated society.[10] Much of this effort was spurred by the urban racial element of immigrants who valued a commitment to social welfare policies. Initially, the new direction was opposed by the South. However, The Great Depression and the election of Franklin D. Roosevelt, bringing his New Deal to the forefront of American politics, did much to invigorate the party's commitment to advocate for rights of the outgroup. That commitment was a major issue in the move of African-Americans from the abolitionist Republicans to the traditionally racist Democrats.

Softening of Democrats on the race issue enthusiastically won African-Americans over. Many were cautious at first, but once the New Deal began to take shape they all but totally abandoned the Republican party. In the aftermath was a Democratic political domination for more than 30 years. In addition, by the efforts of Southern populists and Northern liberals, Democrats were able to control Congress for all but four of the 48 years between 1933 and 1981.[11] While President Harry Truman may have suffered some dislike on the part of Euro-Americans, because of his refusal to support harsh racial policies he won reelection in 1948, running on the same New Deal that was first popularized by Roosevelt. Following Truman, war hero Dwight D. Eisenhower took the White House in 1952, but Democrats maintained control of Congress for six of his eight years in office.[12]

By the post-1960s presidential nomination of a Southerner, Jimmy Carter, it would have appeared that race would be a secondary force in driving American politics. However, Carter was not the typical Southern Euro-American racist in that his support of and by African-Americans was well known. As a result, his presidency and the Democratic political hold were weakened, given the racist overtones of many Euro-American citizens. Some felt African-Americans had gotten more in the way of their issues than merit would warrant. The resulting contradiction in values in association with emerging issues such as affirmative action encouraged many Euro-Americans to turn to the Republican party, where conservative and racist elements were finding welcome. David Duke, without making overt reference, was a bold statement on the racist direction of the modern day Republican Party.

In 1999, David Duke, a Louisiana Euro-American who was associated with the Ku Klux Klan, ran as a Republican for the seat of Rep. Bob Livingston (R-LA). Duke, also a neo-Nazi sympathizer, was a major embarrassment to the GOP because he did not adhere to its race code by being too overtly racist. Despite his known bigotry Duke had been the Republican Party's choice in 1990 to defeat a then-incumbent Democratic Sen. J. Bennett Johnston. Soon after, Duke ran against and defeated the Republican Gov. Buddy Roemer in the gubernatorial primary. As Republican Party nominee, Duke eventually lost to the Democrat Edwin W. Edwards.[13]

As an overt racist and Republican, Duke put the Republican Party in a vulnerable position. Party officials repudiated him at every opportunity in an effort to distance themselves by openly supporting his Democratic opponents. They knew that he frightened many moderate Euro-Americans with his race hatred and could not afford to lose their vote if they wanted to win elections. In fact, the Republican Party made an official effort to distance itself from Duke's rhetoric.

Duke's Republican aspirations assured national press attention. That attention focused on a run for the Republican presidential nomination in 1992. Four years later, in 1996, Duke took part in a close primary election for the U.S. Senate. The state of Louisiana has a rather peculiar election process in that both Democrats and Republicans run in the same primary. If no one manages 50 percent of the vote, the two leading candidates have a runoff. Hence, the larger candidate pool increased the likelihood of a Duke victory.[14] Win or lose, Duke had firmly established the modern day Republican Party as a racist element, which it publicly denies.

The landslide victory election of Ronald Reagan to the presidency in 1980 represented a new Republican party. Where the party was once the voice of African-Americans and others, including women, its new direction recognized their issues as nearly irrelevant. Unlike Duke, Reagan never voiced any disregard for race, but he was by actions obviously in opposition to most racial issues. His strategy was to ignore racism completely as a factor in public life, which gave racists such as Duke a vehicle for posing legislation and other policies that would turn back the clock on gains made previously.[15] "Special interest" became the code for African-American programs. Monies from Washington to local municipalities were now administered via block grants, which put control in the hands of governors who (if Republican) might use such monies for other purposes.

George H. W. Bush was Ronald Reagan's Vice President who, after two successful terms, ran for president himself. Carrying forward with the softer racist policies of the Reagan administration, Republicans maintained control of the White House in the election of Bush senior, who would be a one-term president. Like Reagan, Bush never made an issue of race in his political rhetoric, but race was particularly obvious during his election campaign, in the stereotype exploitation of an African-American convict named Willie Horton.

Following World War II television replaced radio in popularity. Its moving pictures brought images to life in a way that print or radio could not. More than any other component of modern media, television is by far the most potent vehicle for stereotypes. Since the advent of cable television, virtually every home across America has access to its programming. More so than print and radio, television is intimate. Its ability to drive home the stereotype of the African-American male was politically exploited, during a presidential election year, in the person of Willie Horton.[16] Mr. Horton had been let out of prison where he had been incarcerated for rape. There was nothing new about this old stereotype, but the "virtual reality" of television allowed viewers to "pseudoexperience" Horton. It was assumed that citizens, both male and female, would then go out and vote accordingly. At any rate, George H. W. Bush, whose election team had exploited the image, did in fact win the 1988 presidential campaign.[17] Bush's political downfall was brought on by the economy. The Reagan "trickle down" economic theory proved little more than an effort to put money that would normally be reserved for social programs to assist African-American and other disenfranchised groups back into pockets of the wealthy. The obvious failure hurt the Republican's bid for re-election, thus making way for the election of a Democratic White House in the person of Bill Clinton.

William Jefferson Clinton was elected president in 1992 and, as a Democrat, regained the presidency after 12 years of Republican control. His first objective was to improve the economy, which the Reagan and Bush administrations had completely ruined by serving the interests of the wealthy. With the help of Albert Gore—his Vice President—Bill Clinton revived a damaged economy and brought record success in deficit reduction, stock market gains, and the number of jobs created.[18] He was elected to a second term, but the issue of race, though still not uttered by Republicans publicly, was no less potent in the mind of many Americans, especially conservative, right-winged Euro-Americans who were vehemently opposed to his efforts. Thus, as much as Clinton was disliked by some among Euro-Americans he was revered by African-Americans. In fact, African-Americans regarded him affectionately as the first "Black" president. Although Euro-Americans benefited no less than African-Americans from the Clinton years, race with respect to Euro-Americans was more significant. They would be hard pressed to attack Clinton's administration on traditional presidential issues so they looked elsewhere to ensure the defeat of Clinton's Vice President, Al Gore, in his bid for the presidency. They did so ironically on the grounds of "moral" superiority.

Bill Clinton had established himself as a president who was too close to the African-American community, which his detractors repeated in code as "special interest." In 1998, his conservative adversaries got word of his alleged affair with a 24-year-old White House intern named Monica Lewinsky. Embarrassed and wanting to avoid shaming his family, Clinton initially denied the affair. The Republican majority had found a vehicle to denigrate Clinton despite his successes as president. He was eventually impeached in the Republican House of Representatives, but the Senate failed to remove him from office because it could not muster the 67 votes required by law. The scandal disheartened the Democrats, but the mean spiritedness—and some would say racist—efforts of conservative Republicans actually helped the Democrats to gain seats in the House and avoid losses in the Senate during an off-year election.[19]

Republican and/or conservative attempts to smear Bill Clinton for political gain is a caricature compared to Richard Nixon's Watergate scandal. Nixon, a Republican president, died without acknowledging the seriousness of his crimes. The embarrassment he caused the Republican Party made it difficult to debate the Democrats on moral grounds, which they had attempted to do via liberalism. However, the infamous Lewinsky scandal though pales in comparison. The Speaker of the House, Newt Gingrich, once earned his living as an historian and insisted that Clinton's various controversies were much more serious than Nixon's Watergate. While Clinton no doubt engaged in behavior unbecoming a president, Nixon had taken part in an unprecedented number of dangerous abuses of power. Thus, factual historians note not only the Watergate scandal but the high crimes and misdemeanors committed by President Richard Nixon and his staff from 1969 to 1974. The following is an account of what is known:

On 17 June 1972, while investigating a burglary during the early morning hours, the District of Columbia police encountered five men wearing surgical gloves, carrying tear-gas fountain pens, walkie-talkies, and an abundance of newly minted $100 bills. The suspects were attempting to install electronic surveillance units in the offices of the Democratic National Committee, located in the Watergate complex. On investigation it was discovered that the Republicans had intended to spy on the DNC in an effort to circumvent the will of the people and re-elect President Nixon. They had invested at least $250,000 for counterintelligence in this effort. Some speculate that the damage may have already been done in that the burglars hired by G. Gordon Liddy may have been on their second trip. On this trip, they were, in fact, there to remove or replace electronic units that had been previously planted. Nixon immediately denied any involvement of himself or his staff. His press secretary dismissed the incident as a mere "third-rate burglary."[20] Once all the details became apparent, a host of crimes were revealed that could have completely undermined our democracy and brought down the entire government.

Still defiant, the Republican president resigned his post in August of 1974. It was determined that Nixon had ordered an earlier burglary of the office of Daniel Ellsberg's psychiatrist, Lewis Fielding, to confiscate documents that he intended to use to smear the former Defense Department worker who had given the "Pentagon Papers" to *The New York Times*. Nixon's attempt to contain the Watergate story was motivated by his involvement in the Ellsberg crime, which he could not deny. He stood ready to commit enormous sums of money to sway public opinion.[21]

Nixon's first attempt to cover-up the Watergate crime was to pay the burglars he had hired and promise them clemency. He and his aides raised $350,000 for that effort and insisted if that were not enough he could obtain a million or more dollars if necessary. When the truth began to unravel, Nixon embraced perjury. Being a lawyer himself he advised his closest aides on how to mislead a Senate select committee by repeating "I don't remember; I can't recall; I can't give an honest answer."[22] To further ensure his cover-up, Nixon ordered the White House counsel to keep close contact with prosecutors in the Justice Department who were advising him of their progress.

With a host of devices at his disposal, Nixon might have gotten away with Watergate but for an elaborate secret taping system. He had used such a system in the Oval Office, Camp David, and several other places that were not as easy to determine. This system had been in operation since February, 1971, without the knowledge of those being taped or many on the White House Staf.[23] Republicans were so effective in minimizing the seriousness of Nixon's crimes as to sway a jaded public to equate them with Clinton's sexual affair hence claiming moral superiority.

Via an assumed morality, a very vocal and active right-wing element of the Republican Party worked with enthusiasm to help defeat Vice President Al Gore and to elect George W. Bush—son of the former President G. H. W. Bush. Despite Bush's arrests for drunk driving (which he tried to conceal) and the arrest of his daughters and his alleged cocaine abuse, the Republicans continued to assume moral superiority over the Democrats. Frequent appearances at church gatherings helped make the assumption palatable. Thus, in perhaps the closest election ever, a Bush Supreme Court was able to decide in favor of electing the junior Bush as President by disqualifying the votes of African-Americans in several Florida districts. The plan had been put in place some time before voters went to the poles on Election Day 2000. In a previous summer, Bush's campaign co-chairperson, Katherine Harris, hired Database Technologies to scrutinize the voting roles for African-Americans who were "suspected" felons with the intent of denying their participation. Bush's brother, Florida governor Jeb Bush, whose wife was involved in a felonious $19,000 jewelry fraud and whose daughter was drug addicted, cooperated in that effort. In fact, the company hired by Harris removed not only African-American felons from Florida's voting roles but thousands of African-Americans who were otherwise qualified to vote.[24] Such a political effort was unprecedented and did not limit discrimination to race. Thus, Republican racism, though still coded, was becoming more apparent in their dislike for women, Gays, and any others among outgroups. That dislike was evident despite the fact that Bush's Vice President, Richard Cheney, and past-Speaker of the House, Newt Gingrich, are both from families with lesbian members. Once Bill Clinton had served his term in office and Al Gore defeated, the same element used racial code to attack, denigrate, and otherwise attempt to derail the political career of Clinton's wife, Hillary. Despite their efforts in 2000, Hillary Clinton won a Senate seat representing the state of New York.

The history of politics in America is a product of race. From America's initial involvement in the slave trade to its "Emancipation Proclamation" of African-descended citizens, race permeates the totality of its institutions. Thus, while human bondage is illegal and the status of African-descended Americans has been elevated to that of all others, their current status among politicians is no less an extension of the bondage that made emancipation necessary. Their behavior and values remain racist, but less overt than in the antebellum. One of the most salient examples of this behavior was in the comments of Mississippi Senator Trent Lott.

In the heat of a Republican takeover of Congress, a Pennsylvania group of labor, religious, community, business, and advocacy organization leaders called on their Senator, Arlen Specter, to move on the demotion of Lott as Senate Majority Leader. Lott had commented about the frustration he felt about racist Strom Thurman not having been elected when he ran for President in 1948. The group took issue with a history of such comments attributed to Lott. In an attempt to rid the Republican Party of its racist reputation, it was felt that Lott was no longer fit to hold the office of Majority Leader. According to John Hanger, one of the group's members: "The pattern of his own words, his associations and his votes prove beyond a reasonable doubt that Lott is unfit to serve as majority leader."[25] In response, Senator Specter released a statement on Wednesday, 11 December 2002: "I know Trent Lott very well from working with him in the Senate for the last fourteen years and can vouch for the fact that he is no supporter of Senator Thurmond's 1948 platform. His comment was an inadvertent slip and his apology should end the discussion."[26] However, Hanger representing the group felt that Lott's comments were a mere reflection of his bigotry manifested in his voting record. Many of those votes were a direct contradiction to the philosophy of the original Republican Party. Included are the following examples: In 1982 and 1990, Lott cast a vote to derail the Voting Rights Act. In 1990, he voted against the maintenance of the 1964 Civil Rights Act. In 1983, Lott voted down a national holiday for the slain African-American Civil Rights leader Martin Luther King, Jr. What is more, in 1994, Lott voted to defer monies from the Martin Luther King, Jr. holiday commission. Most overtly indicative of racism, in 1981, Lott joined an effort to maintain Bob Jones University's tax exempt status. The University had been noted for its official policy of racial discrimination.[27] Those Americans of African descent, who were otherwise qualified, were not permitted to attend the University. In a bold statement Lott insisted that "racial discrimination does not always violate public policy" despite the American Constitution.[28]

Aside from public comments and his voting record, Senator Lott was an active participant in racist groups. In one keynote address to the Conservative Citizens Council, Lott reiterated that "they stand for the right principles and the right philosophy."[29] The Conservative Citizens Council is a group known to adhere to the philosophy and principles of "white supremacy." They oppose the interracial marriage of American citizens and immigration of those to the country who are not of their racial heritage. Despite such overwhelming evidence of Lott's racism Senator Specter insists Lott is not unfit to serve in the role of Republican leadership.

Ample evidence exists to declare the modern day Republican Party as racist where the political objective is to sustain persons of European descent at the expense of all other races. The actions of Senators, such as Trent Lott from historically antebellum Mississippi, provide dramatic illustrations. However, documentation suggesting that the Republican Party is in any way more or less racist than Democrats is not available. In fact, the Republican Party was founded on the bases of racial fairness and defense of African-Americans who had just recently been released from bondage. Indeed, the Democrats were founded on the bases of all in contradiction to the genesis of the Republican Party that would have institutionalized slavery, kept women in servitude to men, and all but legalized "white supremacy." Thus to associate race with the Republican Party can only be validated at a particular point in time such as the present. At any other future interval the Democratic Party could likely be accused of the same misgivings about race as are Republicans today. That is because dynamics of the American body-politic are driven by race. Subsequently, in the aftermath of slavery race has become the harbinger of Western civilization. Until such time the country can rid its institutions of race prejudice the politics of race will be little more than a cyclic phenomenon among the various political parties.

VIII

Racism in the 21st Century

Racism, according to Banton, refers to the efforts of a dominant racial group to exclude a dominated racial group from sharing in the material and symbolic rewards of status and power.[1] It differs from the various other forms of exclusion in that qualification is contingent on observable and assumed physiological traits.[2] These traits imply the inherent superiority of dominant racial groups that are then rationalized as a natural order of the biological universe.[3]

The most zealous proponents of racism profess that lighter-skinned Caucasian racial groups are superior to darker-skinned non-Caucasian racial groups, i.e., people of color, as a matter of fact.[4] They postulate that they alone have been endowed with the capacities necessary to bring about civilization. So-called "advancing civilization" was a thinly veiled form of racism devoted to rationalizing the right of Europeans to embark on a worldwide mission aimed at conquering people of color.[5] By way of conquest and colonization, Europeans left no terrain of the Third World untouched. After centuries of domination, the mission to "civilize" non-Europeans has necessitated a universal, almost mystic belief in the power of skin color to elevate or taint.[6]

Consequent to differentiations in color, racism has prevailed as one of the most subtle, but no less devastating, and tenacious social problems in the modern era.[7] Volumes of literature have contributed little to any demise of consequence. Germane to the American version is the evolution of the black/white dichotomy, i.e., African-/Euro-American. The black/white dichotomy by definition is predicated on the notion that racism manifests as discrimination by Euro-Americans particularly against African-Americans.[8] There should be no doubt about the importance of this assumption. Conversely, notwithstanding current levels of group diversity, to characterize racism in such a narrow context does disservice to the scientific method. It enables the absurd rhetoric of hierarchy within a single species and in fact provides a conduit for the continued social, economic, and political oppression of dark-skinned people. However deserving of sympathy, the role of victims cannot be ignored. While investigating their undertaking may not be popular or "politically correct," to do so regardless is what distinguishes science from quackery.[9]

Among people of color, manifestations of racism are a direct result of Caucasian race domination. Domination by Caucasians allowed for the exportation of Eurocentric values, which people of color internalized. As it pertains to skin color, the uppermost in status became those who most approximated that of Europeans and the least being an opposite extreme.[10] In an attempt to circumvent humiliation, people of color conformed to the denigration of dark skin. Their efforts necessitated a value system that is in many ways not only physiologically alien but psychologically brutal.[11] The result is a configuration of racism whereby color-based discrimination between people of color extends from the black/white dichotomy. Under the circumstances those who are darkest suffer the most acute instances of discrimination. i.e. racism in the 21st century.

It is imperative in the analysis of racism to comprehend the intimate dynamics between skin color discrimination and power. In the absence of power, the perpetration of discrimination becomes ineffectual. Associated with power, discrimination perpetuates the dominance of one group over another. Thus, it becomes compulsory that dominant groups maintain superior numbers, cohesion, and resources.[12] Light-skinned people of color may lack numerical superiority, but in fact are their descendants, i.e., mulatto, Eurasian, etc.[13] They are cohesive and have access to the control of resources. As a result, they have power. Those of darker skin among people of color may profess numerical superiority but are less cohesive and lack control of resources. Therefore, they are powerless by comparison.

Racism among people of color prevails because it is ubiquitous and historical. The longevity of its manifestation preceded the American sovereignty. Hence, Nicaraguan forefathers considered skin color to have an influence on the manner in which common folk interacted. Mestizos (the racially mixed) refer to the darker-skinned Costenos (persons of African descent) in derogatory terms.[14] For Cuban-Americans, the idealization of light skin has existed historically despite the attempts of Castro's Revolution to eliminate it. Status in Cuba is continually based on gradations of skin color and affects all aspects of Cuban life, both covertly and overtly.[15]

Following their conquest/domination by Europeans, migrants from India, Pakistan, Bangladesh, and Sri Lanka constantly seek ways to prove themselves "white" once they settled in America.[16] In the process, vehement forms of racist discrimination are acted out against dark-skinned citizens, particularly African-Americans.

Perhaps the most dramatic manifestation of racism in the 21st century is "brown racism." According to Washington, brown racism is perpetrated by Mestizos, Chinese, Filipinos, and South Asians against Americans of African descent.[17] It is considered a variation of "white" racism that probably occurred as a result of European conquest/domination.

As for people of color in America, dark skin then necessitates stigmatization.[18] It is a potent and salient feature because it contrasts with that of the dominant group norm.[19] Dark skin may affect on mate selection, stereotype, treatment by the judicial system, and accusations of discrimination by one minority group against another.[20] It is a "master status," which differentiates those so characterized as an inferior element of the population.[21] As a result, people of color develop disdain for dark skin because the disdain is a residue of European racism.[22]

A cursory review of the literature affirms a critical bias in the analysis of racism.[23] Not only are Euro-Americans consistently regarded as perpetrators but African-Americans are consistently regarded as victims. Nevertheless, others suffer similar victimization.[24] In fact, "people of color" is a political construct that includes an ever-expanding assortment of races and their color variations as augmented by increased levels of miscegenation. Such miscegenation among an indistinct population requires that dialogue addressing racism in the 21st century be broadened to discussions that encompass the universe of groups of perpetrators. The most plausible context for an objective analysis is litigation brought by people of color.

Regarding litigation, Title VII of the 1964 Civil Rights Act prohibits employment discrimination on the basis of race, color, religion, sex, and national origin.[25] Following enactment of such legislation, as per the black/white dichotomy, income for people of color rose dramatically. In fact, the earnings of African-Americans surged from 54 percent of those of Euro-Americans to 61 percent in five years.[26] It would appear that progress had become reality. However, that progress did little to address forms of employment discrimination manifested in litigation brought by people of color. It prevails as a testimonial to the likelihood of racism in the 21st century.

Ignorance regarding employment discrimination among people of color is not surprising since the issue is frequently regarded as "taboo" by African-Americans.[27] Among Puerto Ricans, the myth of skin color and racial indifference helps preserve "personalismo" (warmth, openness, and personal attentiveness). Discrimination is made even less conspicuous by the island's nationalistic unity vis-à-vis efforts to gain independence. As a consequence, there is more celebration in social life and courtship among Puerto Ricans than in the U.S., aside from a subtle but tenacious idealization of light skin. Despite this fact, research conducted in 1949 suggested that, although most island residents denied the existence of discrimination, half felt it was better to have light skin regardless of racial heritage.[28] No one felt it was better to be dark. The custom of entertaining dark-skinned relatives in the kitchen, much as servants would have been treated, is a common notion and not unknown to Puerto Ricans who migrate to the U.S. mainland. It implies that some relatives are not as preferred as others, precipitating family schisms.[29]

Travel brochures to the island of Puerto Rico aptly profess the rich variation in skin color and other phenotypes among its people. Vacationing tourists are impressed by the seeming lack of color prejudice, which residents proudly proclaim. Unmentioned, however, is the perception of blatant employment discrimination against dark-skinned Puerto Ricans. Its existence is invisible to the casual observer, but substantiated as fact as illustrated in the following cases. These cases are typological in that they account for charges of skin color discrimination both across and within group and gender lines.

One of the first cases of discrimination litigation brought by people of color was that of the dark-skinned Felix, the plaintiff, versus the lighter-skinned Marquez, the defendant. It was litigated in 1981 by the U.S. District Court of the District of Columbia. Both the plaintiff and the defendant were Puerto Rican employees of the Office of the Commonwealth of Puerto Rico, in Washington, D.C. (OCPRW). The plaintiff alleged that the defendant did not promote her on the basis of skin color discrimination. At the trial, the plaintiff introduced the personnel cards of twenty-eight of her former fellow employees. She testified that, among them, only two were as dark or darker in color than she. All of the other employees in the office, according to the plaintiff, were "white." Other highly credible evidence presented to the court suggested, however, that she might have been in error.

The plaintiff's own skin color, which she described as "dark olive," appeared to the court to be a medium shade. The testimony of the two dark-skinned employees was sought by the court in deciding the case. Of those dark-skinned employees, one did not appear, so the court had no evidence of their color other than the plaintiff's testimony. On the other hand, the second did appear and, although that employee considered their race to be Puerto Rican, their color would cause them to be identified in the continental United States as African-American. Two other witnesses, described by the plaintiff as "white," appeared to the court to be of a shade quite similar to the plaintiff's darker skin. These observations tended to contradict the placement of a rigid line between "white" and "non-white" employees drawn by the plaintiff in her testimony and reflect the fact that a substantial number of Puerto Ricans are of mixed racial ancestry.

Of the twenty-eight employees whose personnel history cards were introduced in evidence, it was apparent that eighteen were office and clerical employees. As with the defendant, the plaintiff was not entitled to a promotion in grade by virtue of her position, her qualifications, her seniority, and/or her length of service. The evidence showed that her employer awarded promotions in grade based on criteria that were neutral, without respect to skin color. Employees whose color was as dark or darker than the plaintiff's were given promotions in grade, while many other employees who were lighter than she were given infrequent promotions, or no promotions at all. Similar neutrality with respect to skin color was evident in the promotions in grade among employees throughout the entire agency. Based on the rules of legal proceeding, the OCPRW did not discriminate against the plaintiff, because of her color, in failing to recommend her for a promotion in grade. Thus, the court decided that the plaintiff was not promoted in grade for legitimate business reasons, having nothing whatever to do with her skin color.[30]

In a more recent case brought by Puerto Ricans on the island of Puerto Rico, *Felero versus Stryker* was litigated in 1998 by the U.S. District Court of the District of Puerto Rico. Falero, the plaintiff, is a dark-skinned male while Rigoberto, the corporation defendant, is a light-skinned male. The plaintiff claimed he was terminated from his job on the basis of having dark skin. The defendant contended that the plaintiff did not establish that he was replaced by someone not within the protected class. The defendant further stated that the plaintiff's job had not been filled by anyone, but admits one of his areas of work was assigned to another employee. Thus, direct evidence of skin color discrimination was lacking.

Absent direct evidence of skin color discrimination, the court took the position that the plaintiff must employ the familiar burden-shifting method enunciated in *McDonnell Douglas Corporation v. Green*. In the first instance, the plaintiff bears the initial burden of establishing a prima facie case of Title VII discrimination. In other words, the plaintiff had to show that (1) he was within a protected class; (2) he was qualified to perform his duties; (3) he was terminated; and (4) he was replaced by a person who was not within the protected class. The burden then shifts to the defendant to produce a valid and non-discriminatory reason for the dismissal. The employer needed enough evidence to enable a rational fact-finder to conclude that a nondiscriminatory reason for the challenged employment action existed. Lastly, the burden shifted back to the plaintiff to show that the defendant's stated reason was but a mere pretext for discrimination. This, in turn, required that the plaintiff proffer enough competent evidence to support two separate findings: that the defendant's reason was pretext and that the true motive was discrimination on the basis of skin color.

In sum, while the fourth element of *prima facie* had been established, the court decided that no reasonable judge of fact could conclude that the defendant discriminated against the plaintiff on the basis of his skin color, based on the evidence in the record when viewed in the light most favorable to plaintiff. Therefore, the court granted the defendant's motion for summary judgment. Additionally, after dismissing the plaintiff's foundational federal claims, the court reassessed its jurisdiction over the supplemental state claims. Thus, in the exercise of its discretion, and after balancing the competing factors, the court declined to exercise jurisdiction over plaintiff's supplemental claims. The plaintiff's state law claims were then dismissed without prejudice.[31]

Perhaps the first discrimination case brought by African-Americans was *Walker versus the Internal Revenue Service* (IRS), in 1989, in the Atlanta Federal District Court. The plaintiff, Ms. Tracy Walker, was a permanent clerk typist in the Atlanta IRS office. The plaintiff was a light-skinned African-American female. Her supervisor, the employee of the defendant, was Ms. Ruby Lewis. Ms. Lewis was a dark-skinned African-American female. The employees in the office in which the plaintiff and the defendant worked were predominantly African-American. In fact, following her termination, the plaintiff was replaced by an African-American. According to the record the working relationship between the plaintiff and the defendant was strained from the very beginning--that is, since approximately November of 1985. The plaintiff contends that the defendant singled her out for close scrutiny and reprimanded her for many things that were false or unsubstantiated. The plaintiff's relationship with her former Euro-American supervisor, Virginia Fite, was a cordial one. In fact, the plaintiff received a favorable recommendation from Fite.

In taking action the plaintiff met with Sidney Douglas, the EEO program manager for the Atlanta IRS district about the problems she was having with the defendant. Two weeks later, pursuant to the defendant's recommendation, the plaintiff was terminated. The reasons given for her termination were: 1) tardiness to work; 2) laziness; 3) incompetence; and 4) attitude problems. It was the plaintiff's belief that the reasons were fabricated and were the result of the defendant's personal hostility toward the plaintiff because of the plaintiff's light skin. The plaintiff did not present any direct evidence that the defendant was prejudiced against light-skinned African-Americans. There was, however, evidence that the defendant might have harbored resentful feelings toward "white" people, and, therefore, by inference, possibly toward light-skinned African-Americans. The plaintiff maintained that she was treated unfairly, for no apparent reason, prior to her termination. She would have the court find that the unfair treatment was due to the defendant's prejudice against her light skin color.

Following her termination the plaintiff filed a lawsuit pursuant to Title VII of the Civil Rights Act of 1964. The plaintiff alleged she was terminated because of invidious discrimination on the part of her supervisor, and that her termination constituted retaliation due to her complaining to the EEO. Given that this was a Title VII action, the case was initially heard before a magistrate. The magistrate recommended granting the defendant's summary judgment motion with respect to the claims under the Administrative Procedure Act, granting the portion of the defendant's summary judgment motion that dealt with the Title VII invidious discrimination claim, and denying the defendant's summary judgment motion with respect to the retaliation claim.

In sum, the federal court ruled on a portion of the magistrate's recommendation that granted the defendant's motion for summary judgment with respect to the plaintiff's 1981 claim, the plaintiff's 1983 claim, and the plaintiff's Administrative Procedure Act claim. The court also adopted that portion of the magistrate's recommendation that denied the defendant's motion for summary judgment with respect to the plaintiff's Title VII retaliation claim. Following my own testimony when called as an expert, the federal court set aside that portion of the magistrate's recommendation that granted the defendant's summary judgment motion with respect to plaintiff's Title VII discrimination claim.

Therefore, the federal court granted the defendant's summary judgment motion as to the plaintiff's 1983 claim, the plaintiff's 1981 claim, and the plaintiff's Administrative Procedure Act claim; and denied the defendant's summary judgment motion as to the plaintiff's Title VII claim.[32] At present, the plaintiff is awaiting the appeal decision of a higher court.

While the aforementioned discrimination litigation has received limited attention in scholarly and journalistic literature, lawsuits by people of color continue to the present date. *Porter versus the State of Illinois* is one such case, recently, in 1997, in U.S. District Court, Northern District of Illinois, East Division. Porter, the light-skinned African-American male plaintiff, cited the

States' statement as direct evidence that race was a motivating factor in his termination. The plaintiff stated in his affidavit that: "During one of my first meetings with Marcia Williams (the dark-skinned female defendant employee) soon after she became my supervisor, she told me that she did not like light-skinned African-American men and that she was going to get rid of me before my probationary period was over." Although the defendant denied that this conversation occurred, she acknowledged that she prefers dark-skinned African-American men as social partners or mates. She also admitted that she discussed this fact with her friends, but she did not recall whether she also shared that information with the plaintiff. The defendant contended that this evidence was immaterial because the record did not reveal any causal link between her statement and the plaintiff's subsequent termination.

The parties did not dispute that the defendant lacked authority to discharge the plaintiff or even to recommend his discipline or discharge. As a matter of state law, final disciplinary authority was vested in the Director of the Illinois Department of Central Management Services. However, there was also evidence that the defendant played a significant role in the decision to fire the plaintiff. As the plaintiff's immediate supervisor, the defendant monitored his work and prepared the negative evaluation of November 1994. She initiated the charges that led to both of his pre-disciplinary meetings, and she conversed with the appropriate administrators who decided whether or not to recommend discipline. Although the record did not reveal the extent to which the final decision-making authorities actually relied on the charges formulated by the defendant, it contained sufficient evidence to raise a factual question about whether she had a significant hand in their decision.

The possibility that the defendant played a significant role in the plaintiff's termination did not imply that her alleged bias was a material factor in that discharge. The plaintiff sought to forge this causal relationship by suggesting that racial animus led the defendant to reject his work, thus saddling him with an artificially inflated caseload or to invent the charges against him.

The plaintiff offered no specific evidence to rebut the charges that formed the basis of his discharge, nor did he cite any evidence other than his own word to show that his work was comparable to that of colleagues who were not disciplined or discharged. The fact that the plaintiff failed to meet his deadlines even after his supervisors reassigned his pending cases and reduced his case intake suggested that he would have been unable to do his job even if the defendant had not returned his work. Standing alone, the plaintiff's own testimony about the quality of his job performance did not discredit the evaluation of his work offered by his employer. Accordingly, the court found that the defendant's statement bore no material relationship to the plaintiff's termination and was not direct evidence of intentional skin color discrimination.

Thus, according to the court, the defendant presented virtually overwhelming evidence that the plaintiff was not performing his job adequately when he was discharged from his job with the State of Illinois. Rather than produce any specific evidence to rebut the charges, the plaintiff relied primarily on his own self-serving testimony to show that his work was adequate. Accordingly, the court found that the record contained insufficient evidence to raise an inference that the plaintiff was fired because of his age, race, or complexion in violation of Title VII, or the Equal Protection Clause of the Fourteenth Amendment.[33] As a result, the defendants' motion for summary judgment was granted.

In the same year, District Court, and state of the Porter case, an African-American male, the plaintiff Lamont Sullivan, was employed as a "supervisor of reel assembly" at the Presstronics facility in Aurora, Illinois, from February 1995 until July 1996. In July 1996, the plaintiff was laid off by Presstronics, ostensibly due to a lack of work at the company. The plaintiff attempted to regain his position at Presstronics in late July, but was informed at that time that he had been laid off indefinitely, and that his employment with the company was therefore terminated. Despite the company's representations that the plaintiff's termination was motivated by lack of work, Presstronics hired less-experienced White and Hispanic (people of color) workers to do the job the plaintiff had previously done. While the plaintiff did not refer to skin color directly as the basis of alleged discrimination, the association of Hispanic with "white" is strong evidence of that assumption. However, the plaintiff failed to prove his case. For that reason, a motion to dismiss the case was granted by the court.[34]

As with the aforementioned cases, existing skin color litigation is brought primarily by Hispanic- and African-Americans. It is an issue for them irrespective of race, ethnicity, and/or gender. However, to assume Asian- and Native Americans do not harbor similar tendencies would profess ignorance of historical fact. The extensive African and European miscegenation characteristic of Hispanic- and African-Americans creates a wider range of skin color variation, replicating the black/white dichotomy. While plaintiffs in these cases failed to legally establish that racism by skin color discrimination among people of color is rife, its imposition on their psyches is without doubt.

Ying Ma represents a classic example of racism in the 21st century, illustrating discrimination against oppressed populations.[35] It is her contention that what is perceived as racism today completely misses the point. She criticizes President Clinton's "Race Initiative" panel for ignoring the real race problem between minority populations. Of particular concern from her perspective is the hatred directed at Asian-Americans by African-Americans who reside in low-income neighborhoods of the inner-city. She draws on her childhood experiences to reach these conclusions.

Ying Ma reportedly migrated from China at age ten. Her family settled in Oakland, California, where crime, poverty, and racial tension were prevalent. She felt out of place by nature of the clothes she wore and her inability to speak English. Her classmates began calling her "Ching Chong," "China girl," and

"Chow Mein." They degraded her culture, language, ethnicity, and race. In her typical Asian way, Ying Ma remained silent.

Eventually, Ying Ma improved her command of the English language, but, perhaps due to her cultural norm, did not respond to verbal insults. Her trips to and from school were a constant effort to circumvent harassment. She endured many insults on her bus ride home, such as spitballs, profanity, and shouts of "stupid Chinaman." The label "Chinaman" was applied to any person who displayed an Asian appearance, such as Vietnamese, Koreans, etc. Unlike the other Asians on the bus who tuned out the insults, Ying Ma took them personally and indicted an entire race of people on into her adulthood based on what she experienced as a child. The fact that light-skinned African-Americans, middle class African-Americans, or other Americans suffered similar insults from the same group did not matter.

Despite the oppression and racism that characterize any impoverished inner-city neighborhood, Ying Ma grew increasingly bitter and outraged by African-Americans. She admits with a pride and arrogance that her fluency in English eventually surpassed that of those who had harassed her during childhood. What is more, she admits to being the object of vulgar sexual remarks, which she contends embarrassed her. This complaint about sexual vulgarities stems from the rhetoric of antebellum racism where southern slave traders sought to demean African-Americans in their stereotype of the "black beast rapist", as if Euro-Americans were incapable of such things.

Ying Ma was not only mindful of the insults hurled at her personally by African-American students but those hurled at other Asians as well. She recalls a middle-aged Chinese vendor, who spoke poor English, in her high school cafeteria. On a daily basis African-American students insulted him with shouts of "dumb Ching!" Ying Ma describes African-Americans who would approach elderly Asians to frighten them with taunts of: "Yee-ya, Ching-chong, ah-ee, unyahhh!" She further takes issue with African-Americans who would insist that her people "go back to where you came from!"

Commensurate with racism in the 21st century, Ying Ma directs her criticisms at "prominent black leaders" who refuse to acknowledge the existence of "black racism." She refers to activists such as Al Sharpton and Jesse Jackson as if she were tutored by their political opponents. Even the world-renowned John Hope Franklin, African-American history scholar and chair of President Clinton's race panel, cannot escape her criticism. She insists that African-Americans such as Franklin complain continuously about racism inflicted by "whites" while completely ignoring that of African-Americans against innocent migrant Asians.

Ying Ma does not limit her attacks to African-Americans. In the spirit of subjugation, she criticizes the leadership of her Asian community as well. According to her, they have failed to act on "black racism" because they fear African-Americans. Describing a rally she attended in New York's Chinatown, Ying Ma had gone to learn about Indonesia's history of discrimination against ethnic Chinese. That discrimination had recently resulted in a wave of bloody anti-Chinese riots. Without prompting, a woman at the rally begin to scream hysterically about her frustrations with African-American racism. The woman's name was Mee Ying Lin. Mee Ying Lin had felt similarly about African-Americans, she hated them. By then, Ying Ma was certain that others had felt just as she felt—that African-Americans, aside from being the victims of racism, were perpetrators as well.

Ying Ma contends that the reason "black racism" is ignored is due to the fact that the Asian leadership is out of touch with the common Asian community. That disconnection is even more pronounced at the national level. A disproportionate representation of the Asian leadership consists of assimilated Asian-Americans whose families may have migrated to America several generations sooner. They have a different perspective and different concerns compared to their more recent migrant counterparts. Furthermore, there may be class, language, and cultural differences that alienate Asian leadership from its yet assimilated counterpart. Thus, they cannot know or understand the critical issues faced by recent migrants because they live comfortable middle-class lives. This disconnect encourages many Asians to then remain silent about "black racism."

Ying Ma is bent on condemning the Asian-American leadership who do not support racist views of African-Americans. She further asserts that it is not a matter of an inability to confront "black racism" but rather a decision not to do so. According to her, some Asian leaders have even attempted to justify "black racism" as a result of competition over limited resources. The most glaring example is when Asian businesses locate in African-American neighborhoods. Boycotts inflamed both sides, like the year-long 1990 Brooklyn, New York, stand-off between the African-American community and a Korean store. Another example involved Korean merchants and occurred in south-central Los Angeles during the 1992 Rodney King riots. While the riots were not directed at Asians initially, the violence soon spread to them, engulfing their segregated community. Ultimately, Ying Ma does not see the economic argument as relevant. It is instead, she contends, a smoke-screen for jealousy against Asian-Americans by African-Americans who view them as better off.

Socio-economic class eliminates any doubt, according to Ying Ma, that "blacks" commit racist acts against Asian-Americans. In the case of San Francisco's Hunters Point public housing complex, which is dominated by African-Americans, low-income Southeast Asian residents, who are in the minority, have repeatedly encountered racial harassment. Racist threats and destruction of property have occurred unchecked for years to the point of almost becoming a norm. Ying Ma cites Philip Nguyen, of the Southeast Asian Community Center, who insists his community has made every effort to get along with and even befriend African-Americans, but to no avail. The problems have remained for ten years or more.

In the spirit of fairness, Ying Ma acknowledges painstakingly that there is some Asian "prejudice" against African-Americans. However, her response is to trivialize it and all but dismiss it as being relevant to "black racism." After all, Asian prejudices, she muses, cannot possibly be that significant because many Asian migrants had never even seen a "black" person before coming to America. Somehow in her formidable intellect Ying Ma dismisses the popular sale of "Darkie" brand toothpaste in Korea, the international criticism of Japan for their denigration of "black" people, and the comments by Japan's Prime Minister that African-Americans are a social problem. More importantly, Ying Ma dismisses historical Chinese culture, which demeaned everything Western and taught the young that all non-Chinese were barbarians, particularly dark-skinned Africans. Subsequently, Asian migrants who had never seen a "black" person prior to coming to America considered them inferior. A cursory review of the research literature complies with this notion.

According to Hogue the most obvious indications of a skin color hierarchy among Asians exists in the attitudes of Northern Asians, including Chinese, Japanese, and Koreans.[36] All three peoples have a significant degree of racial homogeneity within the population. Arguably, it is among the Japanese that the strongest evidence of bias may exist. They have historically maintained myths that rationalize the superiority of Japanese people as an aspect of cultural norm. Thus, the world is composed of the Japanese and their inferior foreign counterparts, referred to as "gaijin." It should come as little surprise that this belief would be relevant to Japan's treatment of non-Japanese, particularly the dark-skinned. They were no less arrogant and brutal than the West in their management of colonial subjects.[37] The Japanese color hierarchy is manifested in a strong sense of superiority, which they apply on the basis of skin color and ranking those who are darkest at the very bottom. The same system is applied to Japanese citizens who may be among Japan's minority group.

In *The Rape of Nanking,* author Iris Chang refers to the cruelty and brutality of the Japanese toward the Chinese during their colonial occupation.[38] However, the Japanese and the Chinese are not so different in their regard for dark-skinned people. Like the Japanese, the Chinese have historically regarded themselves as superior, separate, and apart from the rest of mankind. Any non-Chinese who would welcome the opportunity to stain the purity of Chinese blood are considered barbarians. As a result, when Chinese students traveled abroad to be educated, they were warned by their elders not to return married to a "red-haired devil" whom they did not perceive as human.[39] So-called "red-haired devils" were, of course, light-skinned humans who hailed from the West. Those who were dark-skinned and/or from Africa occupied a rank so far below Western "devils" as not to even be considered worthy of Chinese's denigration. It was apparent in China during a recent rock-throwing incident by hundreds of Chinese students who descended unprovoked on visiting African students.[40]

The remainder of northern Asians consists of Koreans who retain an equally pronounced sense of skin color hierarchy and racial superiority, which is not irrelevant to the King riots in Los Angeles. Many of their cultural beliefs are commensurate with those of the Japanese. According to a survey conducted by *The Far Eastern Economic Review,* Koreans lead all groups in their denigration of dark-skinned persons. Subjects were asked whether their child could marry a foreigner with their blessing. Results indicated that only 30% of Koreans were amenable, compared with 95% of Western Australians and 84% of Filipinos. As might be expected, among northern Asians, biracial offspring are denigrated, and, in Korea, non-Korean spouses are ostracized. Most significantly, the Chinese minority in Korea has been subjected to denigration equal to that of the Korean minority in Japan, making for the most noteworthy accommodation of racism once they migrate to America.[41] Thus, when they arrive accordingly the Ying Ma's of the world object vociferously to "black racism", while all but condoning that perpetrated by the dominant race population.

The latest trend in racism among people of color extends to the social milieu of campus life as perpetrated by African-American women. African-Americans in general, despite being victims of racism, are not immune to engaging in social as well as legal acts of racism.[42] That fact was recently brought to public attention at prestigious Brown University, located in Providence, Rhode Island. There, an African-American male named Ralph Johnson and his Euro-American accomplice, a coed named Rachel Davidson, caused a stir among African-American women on campus. The couple's private decision to date one another resulted in a "wall of shame" list compiled by African-American coeds --a list of African-American men who date Euro-American women.[43] The fact that neither member of the couple engaged any form of behavior that would merit such harassment seemed irrelevant. Euro-Americans who took part in similar types of harassment thirty years ago would today have been expelled from campus, enabled by the support of the entire academic community.[44] The fact that perpetrators today are victims themselves should warrant no less tolerance. For people of color to publicly object when couples decide to date irrespective of race is a form of racism fashioned to suit the objectives of the racist. Whether the perpetrator is of European or African descent their identity must be assumed to be, as it is, irrelevant.

Skin color is compulsory to racism in the 21st century.[45] It substantiates people of color as simultaneous victims and perpetrators. As with the black/white dichotomy, the former is contingent on having dark skin. The latter is a psychological residue of European colonization (46). It thus logically followed that trends in racial diversity today, augmented by increased levels of miscegenation, accommodate a view that America is no longer a homogeneous society. In the aftermath, the black/white dichotomy will become less relevant. This does not negate the pervasiveness of Euro-American racism, but allows for an amplified analysis to include the role engaged by all—including people of color. The ultimate outcome will benefit society by contributing to the knowledge base required for its eventual elimination.

The legal motivation for color based discrimination includes, but is not limited to, money, prestige, property, etc.[47] The ability of the various skin color factions to discriminate against one another is intended to assure a conducive quality of life, as litigation would suggest.

Whilst it is well known that responsibility for the genesis of racism among people of color is derived, at least in part, from Europe, the role assumed by people of color must be acknowledged. If not, the aftermath will enable tolerance of a dual standard that will denigrate the struggles of all, regardless of race and/or color, who made the ultimate sacrifice for bringing racism to an end. Americans of every race would do well to savor the thought in preparation to confront racism in the 21st century.

IX

From Race to Reason

The current state of human evolution as enabled by the sense of sight, allows for the generalization of feces abhorrence onto dark-skinned race groups. This generalization culminates in the association of Negroid groups with dirt.[1] The dark color of dirt conveyed by the sense of sight allows for projections onto Negroid race groups by virtue of their characterization. Such groups are then cast as the physiological embodiment of psychic filth and inevitably denigrated, as in the case of the European slave traders who first encountered Africans.[2]

In the works of Freud, there are few references to the social and psychological potency of skin color.[3] During his era, dark-skinned peoples were discriminated against with minimal consequence. Freud's lack of attention to this psychoanalytically rich phenomenon may have been a reflection of dirt fantasies in which the personal tragedies of dark-skinned people were simply irrelevant to Western scholarship.[4] Heretofore, color-based ideals have been less overt and more covert, lodged firmly in the American subconscious. However, the subconscious fantasies from which ideals are fashioned may in effect be more potent than reality itself. Such fantasies are a form of purification reflected in Western culture's obsession with cleanliness. This obsession was likely unknown among primitives.[5] Dirt in the form of excrement is externalized to the outside world and projected by norm onto dark-skinned people who must then thrive despite its implications. The objective of projection must be from the body to the outside world. If this is true, all things that are viewed as dirty or disgusting represent those aspects of the body and its waste products. Hence the psychological justification of slavery and the idealization of light skin vis-à-vis Euro-American.[6]

Dirt projections onto African-Americans reinforce the most potent forms of racism. It is potent because projection enables domination, preceded by minimal psychological consequence.[7] Akin to the distinction between dirt and purity, denigration of African-Americans by projection also reinforces the stratification of class. Hence, the upper and lower, educated and working, and ultimately light-skinned and dark-skinned. The dominant race group in each dichotomy makes something less than ideal of the dominated. Such classification of dark-skinned people is civilization's method of projecting excrement onto the external environment.

The concept of race is the most potent and divisive construct associated with Western ideals. In American society it permeates numerous facets of life including science, government, politics, and social etiquette. Therefore, American citizens of all so-called races have historically assigned undue potency to its worth. This is so despite the fact that race remains a biological hoax.[8] Its ability to influence the quality and direction of interaction between the various race groups is no less potent today than it was during the antebellum. Subsequently, in an era of increased racial miscegenation the social sciences have begun to consider race in a more urgent and scholarly fashion than in years past.

Given the vast number of bogus race theories, to continue studying race without adjusting for biological fact is to engage in the validation of a fraud.[9] Rather than focus on phenotypes to define race science might be better served by its analysis of skin color vis-à-vis human interaction. In this approach, science will likely enable comprehension of the phenomenon for what it is, i.e., the summation of social interaction among a single species of organism. To assume otherwise will accommodate the mindset and political objectives of an era when race was a mere vehicle to the exploitation and domination of oppressed race groups in particular African-Americans (Negroid). The ability of the nation to meet this challenge will determine the quality of life and perhaps the existence of humanity itself in the 21st century and/or beyond. Thus, focusing on quantifiable skin color as opposed to the pseudo-biology of race will result in less pathological outcomes. This approach will also shift emphasis from the superior-inferior dichotomy to the improvement of "race" relations for the betterment of mankind. It will also place greater responsibility on individuals to act without feeling intimidated by group norms. Suffice it to say that concern for the elimination of human disparities must be manifested in the actions of ordinary citizens toward one another without regard for genetic heritage or other assumed race criteria. Any other response to oppression frees Euro-Americans from ascriptions of any responsibility for racism. Subsequently, racism has evolved into a tradition and would appear to have become a cultural norm. More devastating is the idea that racism is now regarded as passé implicit in the notion that America has become a "colorblind" society.[10] Like all rhetorical demands to end racism, the idea of a "colorblind" society is directed at forces thought to prevent Euro-Americans from being discriminated against especially in the job market and school admissions.[11] Furthermore, with regard to affirmative action, African-Americans remain tainted by accusations of incompetence and inferiority because under a racist system Euro-Americans cannot avail themselves to a struggle that does not involve and/or benefit them personally.

America today is at a unique and exciting point in the history of race and race relations. Beginning with World War II and concluding in the 1960s, there appeared a universal shift in the arrangement of races that had been sustained over centuries. That shift was due to challenging the accepted forms of racial hierarchy that occurred following WWII. Such historical awakening was a result of the dissipation of colonization, apartheid, fascism, and, perhaps most significant of all, the eventuality of the African-American Civil Rights Movement. These and other events called into question "white supremacy" in a way that had not occurred in years past.[12] The outcome associated anti-racism with evolution of the democratic ideal by unprecedented fervor. In consequence is an international support for tolerance and racial equality that had been all but nonexistent. Even so, "white supremacy" remains a potent force in American politics and validation of facts. It is manifested in the rhetoric of "fairness" and "equality" in a "colorblind society."[13] Thus, in conclusion, a new racial politics is evolving along overtly anti-racist lines. Both political parties have taken steps to present themselves as being "colorblind" in the design and conduct of governmental policy. The fact is, however, that, in this "colorblind" rhetoric, racism and inequality are sustained. The exploitation of stereotypes such as Willie Horton and the assumed intellectual inferiority of African-Americans when politically necessary still occur suggesting the superiority of "mainstream" Euro-Americans.[14] This is so despite their insistence that equality between the races has been achieved and that racism no longer exists. Suffice it to say that, regardless of political rhetoric, the age-old and deeply ingrained system of racial supremacy remains a potent force in Western society. In a much more subtle way, this new "colorblind" rhetoric poses greater challenges to racial equality than the overtly racist strategies of the past.

The much heralded "colorblind" society is no less than an unofficial version of "white supremacy." It has succeeded in the denigration of programs such as Affirmative Action, which were designed to bring about racial equality in movement toward a level playing field.[15] The continued difficulty makes it apparent that racial politics drive the Eurocentric status quo. Hence any measure of racial equality that has been attained has proven to be neither stable nor substantial. It follows an unprecedented set of events more complex than ever, which still finds accusations of "ethnic cleansing," and general racial intolerance preceding an equally insidious racial complacency. This complacency sustains a new political disposition where mainstream Euro-Americans are no longer tolerant of "white supremacy," but covertly exploit it when politically necessary.

Therefore, racism is not a mere political abstraction that is reflected passively by culture, scholarship, or its institutions. Nor is it representative of some nefarious Euro-American plot to hold hostage African-American and other people of color. It is rather a distribution of political sensitivity into aesthetic, scholarly, and philosophical texts. It is an elaboration not only of a basic racial distinction but of a perspective.[16] By such perspective, scholarly discovery and/or philosophical reconstruction not only control, but, in some cases, manipulate that which is racially (skin color) different. It is otherwise a discourse that is by no means in a conspiracy relationship with political factions in the raw, but is generated by an uneven exchange with various sources of power. Included, but not limited to, is political power, intellectual power, cultural power, moral power. Indeed, racism in America does not represent the body politic in toto, and as such has less to do with morality than it does with worldly co-existence.[17]

Because racism is a cultural and political fact, it does not exist in some archival vacuum or demented fantasy. Quite to the contrary, it is apparent that what is thought or said about racism follows certain intellectual prescriptions. It is evident by a considerable degree of nuance and elaboration seen as the mechanism of a broad superculture. Thus, most Euro-Americans ignore the reality that a "colorblind" society is advocated in a racially dominated environment.[18] They overlook the explicit connection between that environment and justifications for racism, which keeps "colorblind" rhetoric pure. Any effort at all to address the subject has been perceived as crudely iconoclastic. However, there is no negating the fact that Euro-America in general has avoided the effort of seriously bridging the racial gap between African- and Euro-American citizens.[19] Yet there will remain the perennial escape mechanism of saying that Euro-America is more concerned with activism rather than an ideological analysis. In other words, the argument can work quite effectively to block the larger and more intellectually threatening perspective. In the aftermath is a form of racism even more elusive than the subjugation of African people by the use of "colorblind" rhetoric.

For example, during the promotion of one of his books, Derrick Bell, now a New York University law professor, paused to comment on the ease with which Euro-American students complain to African-American professors. He reiterated that while substituting for a colleague at the Harvard Law School, students invested ten minutes of class time to complain about the performance of their absent professor. It occurred to Bell that when the professor is an African-American or other person of color, students are more likely to complain, whether such complaints are relevant to the class or not. They feel equally that it is their right to challenge African-American credentials, correct African-American scholars in their fields of expertise, and to complain about African-American professors to department chairpersons. The fact of their differential treatment vis-à-vis African- and Euro-American professors is no doubt racist. The predisposition of Euro-American students at predominantly Euro-American universities assumes a negative impact on the academic careers of people of color. Yet differential treatment of African-American professors at Euro-American universities, though career threatening it may be, is nonexistent among the ideological priorities of mainstream academia. Furthermore, while publications are usually the mainstay of faculty retention and tenure evaluations, university political or financial issues may exacerbate the importance of student evaluations. Euro-American university committees, in assessing professors, require additional evidence to substantiate the competence of African-Americans. Their efforts may be rendered culpable by the application of time-efficient numerical summaries. Such summaries take precedent over written student comments. And rarely, if ever, will those committees acknowledge the empirical data that substantiates the fact that Euro-American students apply a harsher standard for assessing African-American professors than to their Euro-American counterpart.[20] Ultimately, despite being a "colorblind" society as reflected in Great Britain, African-Americans may suffer the harshest assessment of all, given the fact Oxford University has never tenured a professor of African descent that in its one-thousand-year history.

The seemingly less tolerance on the part of a "colorblind" public for racism would appear that Americans are embracing a more humane approach to the hoax of race. Among the notable examples include the upholding of

133

affirmative action, the election of African-American politicians, and a significant increase in the number of interracial marriages. What is more, while immigration of persons from Asia, Africa and Latin America was all but illegal at one point today such movement is a mainstay of the immigration process.[21] These trends in and of themselves are reason for optimism that America—as is the West—is becoming a more racially tolerant society. However, optimism pertaining to tolerance must be tempered with caution. While the acceptance of such heinous acts as the lynching of African-American men no longer fits the American cultural terrain the structures of society have been less apt to change. Simply put, the institutions of power that were historically assigned to the benefit of Euro-American males in particular are as potent as ever. Such potency is evident in Congress, the board rooms of corporate America, and the continued distribution of wealth along racial lines. These disparities, as McIntosh refers to them, are "white privilege" and operate without the deliberate conscious involvement of well-meaning citizens.[22] Subsequently it is a fact that the most egalitarian of Euro-Americans who are socially inclined to African-Americans contribute to the preservation of their racial group's dominance, enabling "white privilege." Ironically, in an era of increased racial tolerance people of color, though victims, are not immune to the institutionalization of "white privilege" themselves as in the new wave of African-American conservatives. It is only when this privilege reaches the point of being transformed that Americans of all races, and indeed the world, may begin to consider racism to be a relic of the past.

Because racism is endemic to the institutions of America, including the political, race subjugation is prevelant.[23] The polite facade and moral pretense of mainstream Euro-America destines "white privilege" to a longevity rivaled only by the racism from which it emerged. Thus, those who dare acknowledge its existence prefer to do so in the context of some remote abstraction. They are instructed by cultural experience to ignore "white privilege" much as males are taught to ignore the advantages of gender. Their inability to confront it predisposes them to a painful reality. Germane to that reality is an elusive collection of inherited assets that assigns racial advantages to Euro-Americans over people of color.[24] As a result, Euro-Americans necessarily perceive racial issues via contrasting priorities with people of color and cannot acknowledge their own role in sustaining an otherwise racist culture. Thus, racial issues become secondary because, in the end, the concept of race is beneficial to Euro-Americans both politically and otherwise.[25]

As humanity moves toward a more global community into the 21st century, the issue of race will evolve but also will remain no less potent pertaining to the dynamics of politics. The future of our species might very well depend on its ability to resolve the racial dilemma in an effort to bring about fewer racist practices and policies. This means that the viability of humanity also depends on how the concept of race is acknowledged in racism. Existing terrorism including a renewed tendency toward religious exaggeration, worldwide poverty, and otherwise Balkanization, cannot be managed or even comprehended without engaging a conceptual tool that will make it possible, i.e., skin color.

Skin color in America is a subtle criteria of racism that has had an impact on the nation throughout its history.[26] This otherwise obvious assumption is not in the least subject to challenge. Skin color no doubt represents a recapitulation of the present world-order, which has been dominated by a Western geo-political structure since Europe's colonial imperialism. Thus, until 1945, science was centralized in the West. This included France, Great Britain, Germany, Italy, and the United States, further validating the concept of race. Moreover, despite the globalization of knowledge, science remains a bastion of Western operatives.[27] Commensurate with these operatives, modern thinking evolved in correlation to Eurocentric problems, Eurocentric perspectives, and Eurocentric concepts. Thus, it was virtually inevitable that the ability of "scholars" to think critically would be impacted. That impact reflects the Eurocentric constrains within which thinking has occurred. As per Western standards, skin color has been subsequently trivialized by Eurocentrism. Eurocentrism is a modern demonstration of hegemony. It is clear that this nation cannot remain viable if continually directed by the influences of race and other Eurocentric constructs.[28] Therefore, it is vital to re-evaluate these constructs after a greater study of their essential meaning. Furthermore, in an era of increased racial diversity, improvements will require commensurate changes in the validation of facts.[29] Changes will allow for deviations from race and similar constructs deemed less relevant to racially similar but otherwise distinct populations. For example, Asian-Americans of Chinese and Cambodian descents are obviously identical in racial category: both frequent a common existential space, and both rely on nourishment from that space to evolve. However, Cambodians and Chinese may differ in skin color hence a different American social experience. Thus, the problem in racial category is that Americans may have much in common, but may evolve from different social heritages that are critical to their well-being.

Therefore, analysis of commonality in some respects may co-exist with contrasts in others. In regard to people of color, the universal application of racial constructs would be in error. The most obvious consequence of this error has been a tendency to underestimate the stresses of non-racial constructs on people of color, because there is no analogous impact on Euro-Americans, i.e., Eurocentrism. As a result, research on people of color is less accurate than research on Euro-Americans because it misses an essential component of their existential experience. In the hyper-utilization of race, people of color are less served, and that disservice is an outgrowth of Eurocentric principles.

In the aftermath of Eurocentric principles, Western institutions have become arguably marketing outlets of Eurocentric thought and existential experiences.[30] This pronounced contradiction between the ethos of modern thinking and the experiences of an increasingly diverse color population has mandated profound challenges to its current structure and ideological configuration. In order to remain viable in a diverse population era, science must accommodate flexibility in thinking to facilitate emerging trends in population shifts. The inability to do so will encourage accusations of elitism from the very populations it proposes to serve.[31] The unforeseen implication of this elitism is that knowledge will convert to something myopic in both shape and substance. It will then lend itself increasingly to the auspices and/or influences of Eurocentric standards of efficiency.[32] In an effort to succeed, the validation of race will be sustained by the pressures of Eurocentric forces. Considering skin color is an effort to enhance reason by re-framing racism to accommodate the interacting analysis of Western populations.

Following WWII and the colonial liberation of Asia and Africa, the consciousness of non-European people worldwide changed dramatically.[33] This had an impact on modern race traditions. In the aftermath of that impact, racism has been subjected to persistent challenges from people of color.[34] Those challenges are no doubt fundamentally justified in the efforts of activists to evolve in the current era. The script is that skin color must replace race, which has distorted analyses of oppressed populations. The task is no doubt multifaceted and complex. Current population trends will require solutions that break the Eurocentric hold on traditional manner of thought.

In the contemporary era, an identification of knowledge and skills related to human interaction with people of color has become a salient priority for business, social, and political education. As a result, many who would have otherwise been oblivious now seek out literature that can readily educate the individual as to the content and context of racial criteria. Much of that literature is racially skewed with only secondary consideration for skin color. Moreover, skin color has been only slightly covered by the various disciplines, including social work, psychology, counseling, etc. Consequently, it has been problematic for Euro-American students, professionals, and others to ignore the vast literature that is pertinent to race. A move toward the study of skin color will provide a comprehensive yet succinct overview of the dynamics of social interaction that was once assigned to race.

A cursory review of scholarly works attests to a trivialization of skin color notwithstanding its salience among people of color. According to the Social Works Abstracts database 1977-2001, twelve articles have been published on "skin color" in almost a quarter of a century (twenty-four years). In leading social work journals, skin color has been totally ignored in this time period, thereby accommodating its trivialization. In social work textbooks, such as *Human Behavior in the Social Environment* by Zastrow and Kirst-Ashman, the issue of skin color as pertains to people of color is omitted from the Index and the 300-plus pages of text, which compromises its worth as a significant issue.[35] The fact that Euro-Americans dominate social work publication cannot be dismissed as irrelevant to their Eurocentric perspective. While they may be cognizant of the critical issues pertaining to people of color, as publishers and authors it is they who determine the priority of what reaches publication. The knowledge that is disseminated then determines the direction and accuracy of the social work knowledge base. What is omitted otherwise ceases to exist. Given the color-based litigation, suicide, contrived marital patterns, and discrimination by and among people of color, these omissions are tantamount to the most blatant distortions of knowledge in toto.[36]

When the individuals of various race groups congregate, any number of unique and sometimes unpredictable patterns of behavior occurs. These patterns are not localized to America but can occur throughout the world. On the other hand, America is comprised of numerous racial and ethnic groups, differentiated by history, immigration, and particular problems. The history, immigration, and problems associated with each group more often than not dominate political discussions and policy debates. Euro-American politicians concerned about racial and ethnic relations, though well intended, may harbor deeply held convictions about policies such as Affirmative Action, from which neither they nor their constituency can find immediate gain. What is more, many social scientists and other scholars desire to understand the problems attributed to race and racial differences in a world that has become vastly more multicultural. This interest is critical to equality, but it presents a formidable challenge in posing consistency in sociological facts.

The ability of humanity to advance from race to reason is contingent on meeting the challenges, consequences, and implications of the fallacy of race. Scholars have generated enormous volumes of literature and empirical evidence to assist in that effort. Thus, scholars now know much more than in years past pertaining to the various populations that differ by skin color, hair texture, and eye shape. This makes it more possible to differentiate between myth and fact. For example, many Americans assume African-Americans are genetically predisposed to intellectual handicap although legitimate research, unlike eugenics in the past, does not support that assumption.[37] Additionally, human interaction on an individual level must begin to adhere to social as well as institutional norms that are conducive when skin color is a significant issue.

Following the turn of a new millennium, the ability to accurately perceive, conceptualize, and interact with people of color is a necessity in a rapidly changing and complex world. In order to enhance harmony and reduce the threats of dysfunction, Americans and other concerned citizens of the world must acknowledge that all groups have assets, capacities, and strengths that should be reinforced. Since many of these assets, such as cultural technologies, are derived from cultural legacies, persons must increase their knowledge base considerably. Furthermore, at a time of more frequent contacts between the world's various populations, scientists are confronted by issues and perspectives that did not require consideration in the past.[38] They are thus challenged in future research to develop creative constructs such as skin color less confined to race. That consideration must remain consistent and viable without interruption to sustain the integrity and prestige of scientific endeavor.

In the lives of most citizens, especially urban Euro-Americans, there are daily encounters with African-Americans and others whose skin color differs from their own. In particular, Euro-American politicians know intuitively that demographic attributes impact their ability to get elected and advocate on behalf of constituency. Yet many do not have the time or motivation to review the necessary literature that would enable them maximum effort in carrying out their civic duty in a diverse public domain. For those who are older, their social experience and education took place during an era when current literature was less accurate or not-existent. Due to the potential for harm and legal repercussions brought by discussions of color, it is then critical that politicians exercise caution when incorporating skin color into policy. Some aspects of color might appear abnormal and indeed absurd from a racial perspective. For example, among certain "scholars," such as Herrnstein and Murray, race is the determining factor of the disparities between African- and Euro-Americans that have nothing whatsoever to do with racism.[39] In the not too distant past, such persons may have been regarded with clout and esteem where today they are less embraced and/or tolerated. In fact, among said "scholars" race is indicative of evolution. Indeed, those who are Caucasian are assumed to be superior. Thus, for legal as well as practical reasons the suggestion of a new racial concept must resist the inclination to label race phenomena as irrelevant simply because it is racist, unfamiliar, and/or not Western. This necessitates worth in the much-heralded emphasis on diversity. Americans who fail to value diversity not only impair the nation's potential, but they may also alienate the international community whose cooperation is critical.

The American acceptance of the skin color phenomena should not suggest any scientific perfection. Some aspects of color may, in fact, represent racist assumptions as well. Subsequently, skin color phenomena may indeed extend from racism that would otherwise require scientific scrutiny for the establishment of fact.[40] Thus, Euro-American politicians who represent African-Americans and other people of color must be cognizant of their own belief systems and what they convey. Politicians' positions on racism are relevant to setting the tone of American race relations. From those who endorse *The Bell Curve* to those who reject it will impact the social environment in a myriad of ways, but they will impact it nonetheless. Hence, politicians who endorse race may be inclined to overlook skin color in certain beliefs and practices, particularly if there is racial commonality between these politicians and their constituency. Conversely, the politician who acknowledges skin color will view the same policies and practices as a disservice to African-Americans. Those who reject skin color in lieu of race may further unintentionally maximize the role of racism in American life. Subconsciously, by means of their behavior, such politicians reinforce racism by using anti-racist "colorblind" rhetoric.

Lastly, race being less significant among people of color helps to determine their existential reality.[41] Their role in that determination must include the decoding of Eurocentric concepts, illumination of hegemonic inequalities, and other moves to intellectual discourse. Through the prescripts of struggle, their efforts have not been without precedent, but in fact endure as a continuum wedded to the larger construct of Western culture. Scientists, Eurocentrists included, must then become cognizant of their unique role: that of advocating for the accurate assessment of oppressed populations.[42] Enabled by the illumination of skin color, scientists will contribute to an effort to purge Eurocentrism from the Western ethos. The outcome will rescue the evolution of reason from the tyranny of race in an increasingly diverse and complex world.

REFERENCES

CHAPTER 1 – NOTES

1. Kitano, H. (1985). *Race relations*. Englewood Cliffs, NJ: Prentice-Hall.

2. Kovel, J. (1984). *White discrimination: A psychohistory*. New York: Columbia University Press.

3. Herrnstein, R., & Murray, C. (1994). *The Bell Curve*. New York: Free Press.

4. Ibid.

5. Rabinowitz, H. (1978). *Race relations in the urban south*. New York: Oxford University Press.

6. Hacker, A. (1992). *Two nations*. New York: Macmillan.

7. Lieske, J. (1993). Regional subcultures and the United States. *Journal of Politics*, 55, 88-913.

8. Ibid.

9. James, D. (1995). Close the borders to all newcomers. In *Taking sides*. McKenna, G., & Feingold, S. (Eds.). Guilford, CT: Dushkin.

10. Murdock, S. (1995). *An America challenged*. Boulder, CO: Westview.

11. Herrnstein, R., & Murray, C. (1994). *The bell curve*. New York: Free Press.

12. Hacker, A. (1992). *Two nations*. New York: Macmillan.

13. Loury, G. (2000). Twenty-five years of black America: two steps forward and one step back? *Journal of Sociology and Social Welfare*, 27(1), 19-52.

14. Lewis, G. (1978). Role differentiation. *American Sociological Review*, 37, 424-434.

15. Barnette, R., & Baruch, G. (1988). Correlates of father's participation in family work. In P. Bronstein & C. Cowan (Eds.). *Fatherhood today: Men's changing role in the family*, (pp. 66-78). New York: Wiley Interscience.

16. U.S. Department of Labor, Bureau of Labor Statistics. (August 1988). *Employment and earnings*, 35(8).

17. Sotomayor, M. (1971). Mexican-American interaction with social systems. *Social Casework*, 52(5), 316-322.

18. Staples, R. (1981). Changes in Black family structures, the conflict between family ideology and structural conditions. *Journal of Marriage and Family*, 47(4), 105-113.

19. Moynihan, D. (1965). *The Negro family: The case for national action*. Washington, D.C: Office of policy Planning and Research, U.S. Department of Labor.

20. Sotomayor, M. (1971). Mexican-American interaction with social systems. *Social Casework*, 52(5), 316-322.

21. Coleman, M., Ganong, L., Killian, T., & McDaniel, A. (1999). Child support obligations: attitudes and rationale. *Journal of Family Issues*, 20(1), 46-68.

22. Horn, W., & Bush, A. (1997). Fathers and welfare reform. *Public Interest*, (129), 38-49.

23. National Commission on Working Women, (1986). In *Race, Gender & Class*, Davis, L., & Proctor, E. (1989). (p.71). Englewood Cliffs, NJ: Prentice Hall.

24. Reed, R. (1988). Education and achievement of young black males. In T.J. Gibbs, (Ed.). *Young, Black and male in America: An endangered species.* Dover Mass: Auburn House.

25. Blood, R., & Wolfe, D. (1960). *Husbands and wives.* New York: Free Press.

26. Beckett, D., & Smith, A. (1981). Work and family roles: Egalitarian marriage in black and white families. *Social Service Review*, 55(2), 314-326.

27. Scanzoni, J. (1975). Sex roles, economic factors, and marital solidarity in Black and White marriages. *Journal of Marriage and Family*, 37, 130-144.

28. Hanson, W. (1980). The urban Indian woman and her family. *Social Casework*, 61(8), 476-483.

29. Hampton, R. (1980). Institutional decimation, marital exchange and disruption in Black families. *Western Journal of Black Studies*, 4, 132-139.

30. Ibid.

31. Hirschman, C., & Kraly, E. (1990). Racial and ethnic inequality in the United States, 1940 and 1950: The impact of geographical location and human capital. *International Migration Review*, 24(1), 4-33.

32. Hall, R. (1992). African-American male stereotypes: Obstacles to social work in a multicultural society. *Journal of Multicultural Social Work*, 1(4), 77-89.

33. Hosenball, M. (May 17, 1999). It is not the act of a few bad apples. *Newsweek*, 34, 35.

34. Ibid.

35. Staples, B. (May 2, 1999). When the "Paranoids" turn out to be right. *Times Fax*, Editorial, 8.

36. Ibid.

37. Ibid.

38. Ibid.

39. Fried, J. (May 7, 1999). In Louima's first day on stand, he tells of brutal police assault. *New York Times*, A, 1(2).

40. Goldman, J., Toth, J., & Tien, L. (August 19, 1990). 3 found guilty in Central Park Jogger attacks. *Los Angeles Times*, A, 1(2).

41. Sullivan, R. (July 11, 1990). Videotapes are core of Central Park Jogger Case. *New York Times*, B, 3(2).

42. Hall, R. E. (February, 1993). Clowns, buffoons, and gladiators: Media portrayals of African -American men. *The Journal of Men's Studies*, 1(3), 239-251.

43. Ribadeneira, D. (October 30, 1994). Like father, like son—Jeb Bush add evokes Willie Horton. *Boston Globe*, 7(1).

44. Bush, Gore and Willie Horton. (July 15, 1992). *Detroit News*, A, 14(1).

45. Rakowsky, J. (June 30, 1995). Evidence pointed to black suspect, police captain says of Stuart case. *Boston Globe,* 78(1).

CHAPTER II - NOTES

1. Thomas, H. (1998). *The slave trade*. London: Papermac.

2. Ibid.

3. Ibid.

4. Ibid.

5. Franklin, J. H. (1967). *From slavery to freedom*. New York: Vintage Books.

6. Ibid.

7. Stampp, K. (1956). *The peculiar institution.* New York: Vintage Books.

8. Hall, R. (2003). *Discrimination among oppressed populations.* Lewiston, NY: Mellen Press.

9. Thomas, H. (1998). *The slave trade.* London: Papermac.

10. Ibid.

11. Ibid.

12. Ibid.

13. Ibid.

14. Ibid.

15. Franklin, J. H. (1967). *From slavery to freedom.* New York: Vintage Books.

16. Thomas, H. (1998). *The slave trade.* London: Papermac.

17. Ibid.

144

18. Ibid.

19. Franklin, J. H. (1967). *From slavery to freedom*. New York: Vintage Books.

20. Ibid.

21. Lawler, J. M. (1978). *I. Q. heritability and discrimination*. New York: International Publishers.

22. Stampp, K. (1956). *The peculiar institution*. New York: Vintage Books.

23. Ibid.

24. Ibid.

25. Ibid.

26. Ibid.

27. Ibid.

28. Ibid.

29. Ibid.

30. Hall, R. (2003). *Discrimination among oppressed populations*. Lewiston, NY: Mellen Press.

31. Ibid.

32. Ibid.

33. Stampp, K. (1956). *The peculiar institution*. New York: Vintage Books.

34. Ibid.

35. Ibid.

36. Ibid.

37. Ibid.

38. Ibid.

39. Ibid.

CHAPTER III – NOTES

1. Hall, R. (2003). *Discrimination among oppressed populations*. Lewiston, NY: Mellen Press.
2. Ibid.

3. Ibid.

4. Ibid.

5. Ibid.

6. Twesigye, E. (Ed.). (1991). *God, race, myth and power: An Africanist corrective research analysis.* New York: Lang.

7. Stampp, K. (1956). *The peculiar institution.* New York: Vintage Books.

8. Wilson, W. J., (1980). *The declining significance of race.* Chicago: University of Chicago Press.

9. Lawler, J. M. (1978). *I. Q. heritability and discrimination.* New York: International Publishers.

10. Ibid.

11. Ibid.

12. Thomas, H. (1998). *The slave trade.* London: Papermac.

13. Kovel, J. (1984). *White racism: A psychohistory.* New York: Columbia University Press.

14. Ibid.

15. Ibid.

16. Hacker, A. (1992). *Two nations.* New York: Macmillan.

17. Beckett, A. K. (1983). *The relationship of skin color to blood pressure among Black Americans.* Unpublished master's thesis, Atlanta University, Atlanta, Georgia.

18. Hacker, A. (1992). *Two nations.* New York: Macmillan.

19. Hall, R. (2003). *Discrimination among oppressed populations.* Lewiston, NY: Mellen Press.

20. Ibid.

21. Ibid.

22. Ibid.

23. Ibid.

24. Ibid.

25. Ibid.

26. Ibid.
27. Ibid.

28. Gordon, L. (1986). Family violence, feminism and social control. *Feminist Studies*, 12(3), 453-478.

29. Herrnstein, R., & Murray, C. (1994). *The bell curve*. New York: Free Press.

30. Staples, R. (1976). *Introduction to Black sociology*. New York: McGraw-Hill.

31. Ibid.

32. Lindsay, B., Harris, J., & John, I. (1977). Progressive education and the black college. *Journal of Black Studies*, 7(3), 341-357.

33. Urrutia, A. (1994). The development of black feminism. *Human Mosaic*, 28(1), 26-35.

CHAPTER IV - NOTES

1. Hall, R. (2003). *Discrimination among oppressed populations*. Lewiston, NY: Mellen Press.

2. Hubbard, R. (1995). *Profitable promises: Essays on women, science, and health*. Monroe, ME: Common Courage Press.

3. Ibid.

4. Ibid.

5. Ibid.

6. Ibid.

7. Ibid.

8. Ibid.

9. Ibid.

10. Ibid.

11. Ibid.

12. Weyl, N. (1960). *The Negro in American civilization*. Washington, DC: Public Affairs Press.

13. Ibid.

14. Reuter, E. (1969). *The Mulatto in the United States*. New York: Haskell House Publishers.

15. Rabinowitz, H. (1978). *Race relations in the urban south*. New York: Oxford University Press.

16. Stember, C. (1976). *Sexual discrimination*. New York: Elsevier Scientific.

17. Hall, R. E. (Winter, 1995/96). Dark skin and the cultural ideal of masculinity. *Journal of African American Men*. 1 (3), 37-62.

18. Richards, G. (1997). *Race, racism and psychology*. New York: Rutledge.

19. Ibid.

20. Kovel, J. (1984). *White discrimination: A psychohistory*. New York: Columbia University Press.

21. Pieterse, J. (1992). *White on Black*. New Haven, CT: Yale University Press.

22. Ibid.

23. Ibid.

24. Ibid.

25. Reuter, E. (1969). *The mulatto in the United States*. New York: Haskell House Publishers.

26. Frazier, E. (1957). Black bourgeoisie. New York: Collier Books.

27. Foner, P. (1970). *History of Black Americans*. Westport, CT: Greenwood Press.

28. Bernard, J. (1966). *Marriage and family among Negroes*. Englewood Cliffs, NJ: Prentice-Hall.

29. Wilkinson, D., & Taylor, R. (1977). *The Black male in America*. Chicago: Nelson-Hill Press.

30. Mencke, J. (1979). *Mulattoes and race mixture*. Ann Arbor, MI : University Research Press.

31. Bernard, J. (1966). *Marriage and family among Negroes*. Englewood Cliffs, NJ: Prentice-Hall.

32. Frazier, E. F. (1966). *The Negro family in the U.S*. Chicago: University of Chicago Press.

33. Myrdal, G. (1944). *An American dilemma*. New York: Harper and Row.

34. Wilkinson, D., & Taylor, R. (1977). *The Black male in America*. Chicago: Nelson-Hill Press.

35. Hernton, C. (1965). *Sex and racism in America*. New York: Grove Press.

36. Rose, A. (1964). *The Negro in America*. New York: Harper and Row.

37. Myrdal, G. (1944). *An American dilemma*. New York: Harper and Row.

CHAPTER V – NOTES

1. Snowden, F. (1983). *Before color prejudice*. Cambridge, MA: Harvard University Press.

2. Ibid.

3. Ibid.
4. Ibid.

5. Ibid.

6. Ibid.

7. Ibid.

8. Ibid.

9. Ibid.

10. Ibid.

11. Norton, D. (1993). Diversity, early socialization, and temporal development: The dual perspective revisited. *Social Work*. January, Vol. 38 (1), 82-90.

12. Hall, R. (1993). Clowns, buffoons and gladiators: Media portrayals of the African-American male. *Journal of Men's Studies*, 1(3), 239-251.

13. Klineberg, O. (1974). Pictures in our heads, in E. Schuler, T. Hoult, D. Gibson, & W. Brookover, eds. *Readings in sociology*, 5th ed. New York: Crowell, 631-637.

14. Ehrlich, H. (1973). *The sociology of prejudice*. New York: Wiley.

15. Allport, G. (1958). *The nature of prejudice*. Garden City, NY: Doubleday.

16. Lombardo, B. (1978). "The Harlem Globetrotters and the Perception of the African-American Imagery." *The Physical Educator*, 35(2), 60-63.

17. Bogle, D. (1989). *Toms, coons, mulattoes, mammies and bucks: An interpretive history of African-Americans in American film*. New York: Continuum.

18. Charnofsky, H. (1968). Baseball player self conception versus the popular image. *International Review of Sport Sociology*, 3, 44-46.

19. Jensen, A. (1969). How much can we boost IQ and scholastic achievement? *Harvard Educational Review*, 39, 2.

20. Herrnstein, R., & Murray, C. (1994). *The bell curve*. New York: Free Press.

21. Bogle, D. (1989). *Toms, coons, mulattoes, mammies and bucks: An interpretive history of African-Americans in American film*. New York: Continuum.

22. Ibid.

23. Ibid.

24. Ibid.

25. Ibid.

26. Ibid.

27. Nesterby, J. (1982). *Black images in American film, 1890-1954*. Lanham, MD: University Press of America.

28. Leab, D. (1975). *From sambo to superspade*. Boston: Houghton Mifflin.

29. Maynard, R. (1974). *The black man on film: Racial stereotyping.* Rochelle Park, NJ: Hayden.

30. Blake, T., & Dennis, W. (1943). The development of stereotypes concerning the Negro. *Journal of Abnormal and Social Psychology*, 36, 525-531.

31. Steinberg, C. (1980). *TV Facts.* New York: Facts on File.

32. Ribadeneira, D. (October 30, 1994). Like father, like son—Jeb Bush add evokes Willie Horton. *Boston Globe*, 7(1).

33. Bush, Gore and Willie Horton. (July 15, 1992). *Detroit News,* A, 14(1).

34. Tebell, J. (1963). *The compact history of the American newspaper.* New York: Hawthorn.

35. Silberman, C. (1964). *Crisis in black and white.* New York: Random House.

36. Harrison, B. (1989, August). The jogger running for her life. *Mademoiselle*, 122.

37. Martz, L. (1990, January 22). A murderous hoax. *Newsweek*, 16-22.

38. Jones, J. (1981). *Bad blood.* New York: Macmillan.

39. Stember, C. (1976). *Sexual racism.* New York: Elsevier Scientific.

40. Gonzalez, D., & Kantrowitz, B. (1990, July 23). Still shocking after a year. *Newsweek*, 48-49.

41. Rakowsky, J. (June 30, 1995). Evidence pointed to black suspect, police captain says of Stuart case. *Boston Globe,* 78(1).

42. Dexter, P. (1994, Nov. 16). Must the world's Susan Smiths be politically correct? *Detroit Free Press*, 5E.

43. Hall, R. E. (February, 1993). Clowns, buffoons, and gladiators: Media portrayals of African-American men. *The Journal of Men's Studies*, 1(3), 239-251.

44. Devine, P. (1991). Measurement of racial stereotype subtyping. *Personality and Social Psychology Bulletin*, 17, 44-50.

45. Ibid.

46. Hall, R. (February, 1993). Clowns, buffoons, and gladiators: Media portrayals of African-American men. *The Journal of Men's Studies*, 1(3), 239-251.

47. Davis, L. (1991). The Articulation of Difference: White preoccupation with the question of racially linked genetic differences among athletes. *Sociology of Sport Journal,* 7(2), 179-187.

48. Kitano, H. (1997). *Race relations.* 5th ed. Upper Saddle River, NJ: Prentice-Hall.

CHAPTER VI – NOTES

150

1. Hall, R. E. (1996). Occupational aspirations among African Americans: A case for Affirmative Action. *Journal of Sociology and Social Welfare*, 23(4), 117-128.

2. Ibid.

3. Disch, R., & Schwartz, B. (1970). *White racism* (2nd ed.). New York: Dell.

4. Civil Rights Act, 42 U.S.C. 2000 (1964).

5. Hall, R. E. (1996). Hall, R. E. (1996). Occupational aspirations among African Americans: A case for Affirmative Action. *Journal of Sociology and Social Welfare*, 23(4), 117-128.

6. Ibid.

7. Ibid.

8. Graham, H. (1990). *The Civil Rights Era: Origins and Development of National Policy, 1960-1972*. New York: Oxford University Press, 450-76.

9. Kotlowski, D. (1998). *Richard Nixon and the origins of affirmative action*. Historian.

10. Ibid.

11. Ibid.

12. Ibid.

13. Ibid.

14. Ibid.

15. Ibid.

16. Dwight D. Eisenhower to Richard M. Nixon, 4 September 1953, PPS 307. 10, *Richard M. Nixon Pre-Presidential Papers* (hereafter NPPP), Richard Nixon Library and Birthplace, Yorba Linda, California.

17. Nixon to Clarence Mitchell, 29 December 1955, PPS 307.74; Summary of Discussion at the Meeting with Representatives of Organized Labor, 30 April 1957, PPS 307.97.2; "Nixon's Record on job Discrimination," n. d. [1960], PPS 307.164.2, all in *NPPP*, Nixon Library.

18. Nixon to Mitchell, 15 June 1956, FPS 307.85; Robert E. Cushman, Jr. to Nixon, 29 January 1959, FPS 307.128; Margaret Garrity to Agnes Waldron, 25 August 1960, FPS 307.161A; Robert E. McLaughlin to Nixon, 22 January 1960, PPS 307.149, all in *NPPP*, Nixon Library; News clipping, "Three Negroes Obtain Rodman Jobs Here," 30 April 1960, folder: 1960--President's Committee on Government Contracts, box 129, James P. Mitchell Papers, Dwight D. Eisenhower Library, Abilene, Kansas; "Nixon Receives NAACP Report on Bias in Apprenticeship," *News from NAACP*, 25 February 1960, FPS 307.153, *NPPP*, Nixon Library; Minutes of the Meeting of the Government Contracts Committee, 14 September 1953, FPS 307.41, *NPPP*, Nixon Library; Summary of Conference between the President's Committee on Government Contracts and Leaders of

Organized labor, 15 March 1955, 5, FPS 307.56, *NPPP*, Nixon Library; Harry Fleischman to Herbert Hill, 9 November 1960, folder: Negroes--Employment, box 525, Jay Lovestone Papers, Hoover Institution Archives, Stanford University, Stanford, California; "Randolph Says He, Meany Both Oppose Union Bias," *Chicago Defender*, 17 October 1959, folder: Newspaper Clipping File--October, November, December 1959, FPS 307; Summary of Discussion at the Meeting with Representatives of Organized Labor, 30 April 1957, FPS 307.97.2, *NPPP*, Nixon Library.

19. "NAACP Leaders Plead for No Violence; Injuries Mount," *Philadelphia Tribune*, 1 June 1963, 1, 5; "Negro Policeman Hailed," *Philadelphia Tribune*, 4 June 1963, 3; Graham, Civil Rights Era, 188, 278-79; Executive Order 11246, 24 September 1965, Weekly Compilation of Presidential Documents 1: 9 (27 September 1965) (Washington, 1965), 305-9; "A Buzzword Defined," *Newsweek*, 3 April 1995, 24.

20. Karger, H. J., & Stoesz, D. (1990). *American social welfare policy*. New York: Longman.

21. Stout, K., & Buffum, W. (1977). *The commitment of social workers to affirmative action*. [CD-ROM]. Abstract from: ProQuest File: Dissertation Abstracts Item: 1270.

22. Wilson, W. J., (1980). *The declining significance of race*. Chicago: University of Chicago Press.

23. Schwartz, H. (1984). *In defense of affirmative action*. [CD-ROM]. Abstract from: ProQuest File: Dissertation Abstracts Item: 731.

24. O'Neille, T. (1985). *Bakke and the politics of equality*. Scranton, PA: Wesleyan University Press.

25. Lederman, D. (1996, April, 26). Growing Attacks on Affirmative Action. *The Chronicle of Higher Education*, A27, A30.

26. Jones, R. L. (Ed.). (1980). *Black pride in the seventies*. New York: Harper & Row.

27. *Regents of the University of California v. Bakke*, 438 U.S. 265 (1978) Docket Number: 76-811.

28. Ibid.

29. Jenkins, S. (1993). *The socially constructed meaning of skin color among young African-American adults*. [CD-ROM]. Abstracts from: ProQuest file: Dissertation abstracts item: 453.

30. Hall, R. E. (2003). *The bleaching syndrome*. Manuscript submitted for publication.

31. McIntosh, P. (1989). White Privilege: Unpacking the invisible knapsack. *Independent School*, Winter 90, Vol. 49 (2).

32. Vaz, K. (1995). Racial aliteracy: white appropriations of black presence. *Women and Therapy*, 16(4), 31-49.

33. Jones, R. L. (Ed.). (1980). *Black pride in the seventies*. New York: Harper & Row.

34. Hull, G. (1987). Joining together: a faculty student experience in political campaigning. *Journal of social work education*, 23(3) 37-43.

35. Sullivan, M. (1993). Social work's legacy of peace: echoes from the early 20th century. *Social Work*, 38(5), 513-520.

CHAPTER VII - NOTES

1. Meckgop (2003). *The origin of "GOP."* http://meckgop.com/gop.html.

2. Ibid.

3. Ibid.

4. Ibid.

5. Ibid.

6. "Democratic Party," (2003) *Microsoft® Encarta® Online Encyclopedia* http://encarta.msn.com © 1997-2003 Microsoft Corporation.

7. Ibid.

8. Ibid.

9. Ibid.

10. Ibid.

11. Ibid.

12. Greenstein, F. (1980). Eisenhower as activist president: A look at new evidence. *Political Science Quarterly*, 94(4), 575-599.

13. Edsall, T. (1998). David Duke says he'll run for Representative Livingston's Seat . *Washington Post*: http://www.jessiejacksonjr.com/issues/i122198545.html.

14. Ibid.

15. Ibid.

16. Ribadeneira, D. (October 30, 1994). Like father, like son—Jeb Bush add evokes Willie Horton. *Boston Globe*, 7(1).

17. Bush, Gore and Willie Horton. (July 15, 1992). *Detroit News*, A, 14(1).

18. Greenstein, F. (1994). The presidential leadership style of Bill Clinton: An early appraisal . *Political Science Quarterly*, 108(4), 589-601.

19. Miller, H. (1999). Sex, politics, and public opinion: What political scientists really learned from the Clinton-Lewinsky scandal. *Political Science and Politics*, 32(4), 721-729.

20. Small, M. (Nov. 1998). Grounds for impeachment: Nixon, Watergate, and the White House horrors. *USA Today* (Magazine).

21. Ibid.

22. Ibid.

23. Ibid.

24. Moore, M. (2002). *Stupid White men*. New York: Penguin Books.

25. Murphy, R. (2002). *United Pennsylvanians call on Senator Arlen Specter to demand removal of Senator Trent Lott from leadership position*. Harrisburg, PA: PR Newswire.

26. Ibid.

27. Ibid.

28. Ibid.

29. Ibid.

CHAPTER VIII - NOTES

1. Kitano, H. (1985). *Race relations*. Englewood Cliffs, NJ: Prentice-Hall.

2. Wilson, M. (1992). What difference could a revolution make? Group work in the new Nicaragua. *Social Work with Groups*, 15(2/3), 301-314.

3. Minor, N., & McGauley, L. (1988). A different approach: dialogue in education. *Journal of Teaching in Social Work*, 2(1), 127-140.

4. Welsing, F. (1970). *The Cress theory of color confrontation and racism*. Washington, DC: C-R Publishers.

5. Daly, A., Jennings, J., Beckett, J., & Leashore, B. (1995). Effective coping strategies of African Americans. Social Work, 40(2), 40-48.

6. Hyde, C. (1995). The meanings of whiteness. *Qualitative Sociology*, 18(1), 87-95.

7. Hernton, C. (1965). *Sex and racism in America*. New York: Grove.

8. Stember, C. (1976). Sexual racism. New York: Elsevier Scientific.

9. Aro, J. (1995). The authority of reason and passion for science. The rules of sociological method. *Sosiologia*, 32(2), 81-89.

10. Welsing, F. (1970). *The Cress theory of color confrontation and racism*. Washington, DC: C-R Publishers.

11. Keefe, T. (1984). Alienation and social work practice. *Social Casework*, 65(3), 145- 153.

12. Schermerhorn, R. (1978). *Comparative ethnic relations.* Chicago: University of Chicago Press.

13. Russell, K., Wilson, M., & Hall, R. E. (1992). *The color complex.* New York: Harcourt Brace Jovanovich.

14. Lancaster, R. (Oct 1991). Skin color, race and racism in Nicaragua. *Ethnology,* 30, 4, 339-353.

15. Canizares, R. (1990). Cuban Racism and the Myth of the Racial Paradise. *Ethnic Studies Report,* 8(2), 27-32.

16. Mazumdar, S. (1989). Racist Response to Racism: The Aryan Myth and South Asians in the US. *South Asia Bulletin,* 9(1), 47-55.

17. Washington, R. (1990). Brown racism and the formation of a world system of racial stratification. *International Journal of Politics, Culture, and Society,* 4(2), 209-227.

18. Kitano, H. (1985). *Race relations.* Englewood Cliffs, NJ: Prentice-Hall.

19. Hall, R. E. (1990). *The projected manifestations of aspiration, personal values, and environmental assessment cognates of cutaneo-chroma (skin color) for a selected population of African Americans* (Doctoral dissertation, Atlanta University, 1989). Dissertation Abstracts International, 50, 3363A.

20. Sciara, F. J. (1983). Skin color and college student prejudice. *College Student Journal,* 17, 390-394.

21. Farhard, D. (1988). Jung: A racist. *British Journal of Psychotherapy,* 4, 263-279.

22. Anderson, L. (1991). Acculturative stress: A theory of relevance to Black Americans. *Clinical Psychology Review.* Vol. 11(6), 685 702.

23. Garcia, B., & Swenson, C. (1992). Writing the stories of white racism. *Journal of Teaching in Social Work.* 6(2): 3-17.

24. Banerjee, S. (1985). Assortive mating for color in Indian population. *Journal of Biosocial Science,* 17, 205-209.

25. Moakley, J. (1987). Discrimination in employment of handicapped. *Congressional Record,* Daily ed. 25 Feb 1987, E612-613.

26. Cross, T. (1987). *The Black power imperative.* New York: Faulkner Books.

27. Russell, K., Wilson, M., & Hall, R. E. (1992). *The color complex.* New York: Harcourt Brace Jovanovich.

28. Montalvo, F. (1994). Chicano phenotype and depression. *Hispanic Journal of Behavioral Sciences,* 16(3), 296-306.

29. Levine, E. S., & Padilla, A. M. (1980). *Crossing cultures in therapy.* Monterey, CA: Brooks/Cole.

30. *Felix v Marquez,* 78-2314, (U.S. Dist. Dist. of Columbia, 1981).

31. *Falero v Stryker*, 10F Supp. 2d 93 (U.S. Dist. Puerto Rico 1998).

32. *Walker v IRS*, 713 F Supp. 403 (U.S. Dist. Ga. 1989).

33. *Porter v State of Illinois*, 987 F Supp. 667 (U.S. Dist. Ill. 1997).

34. *Sullivan v Presstronics*, 96 C, Supp. 7436 (U.S. Dist. Ill. 1997).

35. Ying Ma, (1998). *Black Racism: the hate that dare not speak its name.*
    http://www.theamericanenterprise.org/taend98c.htm.

36. Garrett, K. (1999). *Are Asians racist?* http://www.abc.net.au/rn/talks/bbing/stories/s36894.htm.

37. Chang, I. (1997). *The rape of Nanking.* New York: Penguin Books.

38. Ibid.

39. Garrett, K. (1999). *Are Asians racist?* http://www.abc.net.au/rn/talks/bbing/stories/s36894.htm.

40. Washington, R. (1990). Brown racism and the formation of a world system of racial
    stratification. *International Journal of Politics, Culture, and Society*, 4 (2), 209-227.

41. Ibid.

42. Hiskey, M. (1990, February 1). Boss: Skin hue, firing unrelated. *The Atlanta
    Journal-Constitution*, 1, 4.

43. Gose, B. (1996, May). Public debate over a private choice. *Chronicle of Higher Education*,
    A45, A47.

44. Wolf, C. (1992). Constructions of a lynching. *Sociological Inquiry*, 62(1), 8397.

45. Hall, Ronald E. (October, 1992). Bias among African-Americans regarding skin color:
    Implications for social work practice. *Research on Social Work Practice*, 2(4), 479-486.

46. Schiele, J. (1994). Afrocentricity as an alternative world view for equality. *Journal of
    Progressive Human Services*, 5(1), 5-25.

47. Kitano, H. (1997). *Race relations.* Englewood Cliffs, NJ: Prentice-Hall.

CHAPTER IX - NOTES

1. Bullough, V. (1988). Historical perspective. *Journal of Social Work and Human Sexuality*, 7 (1),
   15-24.

2. Clark, K., & Clark, M. (1947). Racial self identification and preference in Negro children.
   Newcomb & Hartly (eds.). *Readings in social psychology.* New York: Holt.

3. Gould, K. (1984). Original works of Freud on women: social work references. *Social Casework*,
   65 (2), 94-101.

4. Rojek, C. (1986). The 'subject' in social work. *British Journal of Social Work*, 16 (1), 65-77.

5. Bullough, V. (1988). Historical perspective. *Journal of Social Work and Human Sexuality*, 7 (1), 15-24.

6. Gaines, S., & Reed, E. (1995). Prejudice: from Allport to DuBois. *American Psychologist*, 50 (2), 96-103.

7. Stember, C. (1976). *Sexual discrimination.* New York: Elsevier Scientific.

8. Lawler, J. M. (1978). *I. Q. heritability and discrimination.* New York: International Publishers.

9. Ibid.

10. Hacker, A. (1992). *Two nations: Black and White, separate, hostile, unequal.* New York: Maxwell Macmillan International.

11. Hall, R. E. (1997). "Fixing" Affirmative Action: Implications for Diversity Among Social Work Faculty. *Journal of Law and Social Work*, 7(1), 35-45.

12. Kitano, H. (1985). *Race relations.* Englewood Cliffs, NJ: Prentice-Hall.

13. Ibid.

14. Herrnstein, R., & Murray, C. (1994). The bell curve. New York: Free Press.

15. Hall, R. E. (1997). "Fixing" Affirmative Action: Implications for Diversity Among Social Work Faculty. *Journal of Law and Social Work*, 7(1), 35-45.

16. Kass, L. (1997). The end of courtship. *Public Interest*, 126, 39-63.

17. Urrutia, A. (1994). The development of black feminism. *Human Mosaic*, 28(1), 26-35.

18. Hodes, M. (1997). *White women, black men.* New Haven, CT: Yale University Press.

19. Hacker, A. (1992). *Two nations: Black and White, separate, hostile, unequal.* New York: Maxwell Macmillan International.

20. Daufin, E. (1995). Confessions of a womanist professor. *Black Issues in Higher Education.* March, 34-35.

21. Hall, R. (2003). *Discrimination among oppressed populations.* Lewiston, NY: Mellen Press.

22. McIntosh, P. (1989). White Privilege: Unpacking the invisible knapsack. *Independent School*, Winter 90, Vol. 49 (2).

23. Rabinowitz, H. (1978). *Race relations in the urban South.* New York: Oxford University Press.

24. Makkar, J., & Strube, M. (1995). Black women's self perception of attractiveness following exposure to white versus black beauty standards: The moderating role of racial identity and self esteem. *Journal of Applied Social Psychology*, 25 (17), 1547-1566.

25. Bendersky, J. (1995). The disappearance of blondes: Immigration, race and the reemergence of "Thinking White." *Telos*, 104, 135-157.

26. Russell, K., Wilson, M., & Hall, R. E. (1992). *The color complex*. New York: Harcourt Brace Jovanovich.

27. Joyner, C. (1978). The historical status of American Indians under international law. *Indian Historian*, 11(4), 30-36, 63.

28. Reichert, E. (2001). Move from social justice to human rights provides new perspective. *Professional Development*, 4(1), 5-13.

29. Patel, C. (2001). Indigenising social work education: A case study from Baroda. *Indian Journal of Social Work*, 62(2), 197-218.

30. Schiele, J. (1997). An Afrocentric perspective on social welfare philosophy and policy. *Journal of Sociology and Social Welfare*, 24(2), 21-40.

31. Tambor, M. (1979). The social worker as worker: a union perspective. *Administration in Social Work*, 3(3), 289-300.

32. Park, S., & Green, C. (2000). Is transracial adoption in the best interest of ethnic minority children?: Questions concerning legal and scientific interpretations of a child's best interests. *Adoption Quarterly*, 3(4), 5-34.

33. Karenga, M. (1995). Making the past meaningful: Kwanza and the concept of Sankofa. *Reflections*, 1(4), 36-46.

34. Ngozi, B. (1997). The US organization, Maulana Karenga, and conflict with the Black Panther Party: A critique of sectarian influences on historical discourse. *Journal of Black Studies*, 28(2), 157-170.

35. Zastrow, C., & Kirst-Ashman, K. (1990). *Understanding human behavior and the social environment*. Chicago: Nelson-Hall Publishers.

36. Hall, R. (2001). *Filipina Eurogamy: Skin color as vehicle of psychological colonization*. Manilla, Philippines: Giraffe Books.

37. Herrnstein, R., & Murray, C. (1994). *The bell curve*. New York: Free Press.

38. Harvey, A. (1995). The issue of skin color in psychotherapy with African-Americans. *Families in Society*, 76 (1) 3-10.

39. Herrnstein, R., & Murray, C. (1994). *The bell curve*. New York: Free Press.

40. Hall, R. (2003). *Discrimination among oppressed populations*. Lewiston, NY: Mellen Press.

41. Hall, R. (2001). *Filipina Eurogamy: Skin color as vehicle of psychological colonization*. Manilla, Philippines: Giraffe Books.

42. Germain, C., & Gitterman, A. (1980). *The life model of social work practice*. New York, NY: Columbia University Press.

INDEX

abolitionists, 23, 28
Administrative Procedure Act, 115
affirmative action: and college
  admissions, 79, 80, 85, 88, 89;
  and employment, 82, 83;
  legislation, 79, 80, 81-83, 138;
  limitations, 79, 83, 86-87;
  opposition to, 79, 80, 89, 90;
  origins, 80-81, 83; and power, 90,
  129; and race, 79; and racism, 79;
  support for, 133; and unions, 82,
  83-85
Affirmative Action program, 131
AFL-CIO, 84, 85
Africa: genetics of physicality of, 19-
  20, 24-25, 27, 29-30; Hamitic
  tribes of, 30, 31; women slaves,
  22. *See also* Africans; Atlantic
  slave trade; Ethiopia; women
African-American(s), 47, 60;
  assimilation, 10; and "brown
  racism", 109, 118-122; and
  Clinton, 99-100; in Congress, 94;
  employment, 8-9; genesis of, 38;
  as inferior, 60, 129; mixed-race,
  55-63; oppressed, 4, 5; parenting,
  9, 10; population, 7; quality of
  life, 10-11, 18; and racial
  sensitivity, 13; racism, 79, 124;
  and sex-role boundaries, 12;
  stereotypes, 67-70, 72-77;
  unemployment, 9, 82; and unions,
  82, 85; as victims, 110. *See also*
  Atlantic slave trade; mixed race;
  Republican Party; slaves;
  stereotype
African-American women: and
  employment, 11-13; and quality
  of life, 11, 12
African-/Euro-Americans, 107

Africans, 38, 19-28, 29; inferiority
  of, 21, 34-35; as slaves, 19-28, 29
Agatharchides, 65
agriculture: economy and, 34; and
  slaves, 24-25
Alabama, 25, 28
Allport, Gordon, 65, 68
America: evolution of, 6-8;
  immigration to, 7; racial
  composition of, 7
American Dilemma, An (Myrdal), 8,
  53
American Dream, the, 5, 6
Amos n' Andy, 73
Asclepiades, 66
Asia. *See individual countries by
  name*
Asian Americans, 47; and bias, 118,
  122; employment, 118; and
  racism, 119-120, 121; voting
  problems, 102. *See also* Lin; Ma;
  mulatto; skin color; stereotype
Asians: "brown racism" of, 109; as
  inferior, 5, 7; and racism, 122. *See
  also by individual country name;*
  Filipinos; stereotype
assimilation, and racism, 45-46
Atlanta, Georgia, 114
Atlantic slave trade: Africans
  differed from others, 20; African
  sources for the, 19-28, 29; cruelty
  in the, 20-21, 26; history of the,
  19, 20-22, 26, 27; Mediterraneans
  in the, 19, 21-22; and populations,
  22; and racist stereotypes, 67
Aurora, Illinois, 117-118
Australia: mixed marriage in, 123
aversion, 32
Bakke case, 81, 86, 87
Bangladesh, 109
Banton, 46, 107

Bell, Derrick, 131-132
Bell Curve, The (Herrnstein and
Murray), 70, 140
Bennett murder accusation, 17
bias. *See* miscegenation; mulatto;
racism; skin color; stereotype
biracial offspring, 123. *See also*
African-American; Asian-
American; Euro-American
"black", 30, 31, 32, 54-55, 67, 122
"black beast rapist" stereotype, 119
"black racism", 120-121, 122
black/white dichotomy: defined, 45,
107; phenotype, 118; and racism,
107-108, 124
Blake and Dennis, 73
block grants, 98
Boas, Franz, 39-40, 44-45
Bob Jones University, 104
Bogle, Donald, 70, 72
Boston, Massachusetts, 17, 75-76
Bradley, 59
Brazil, 24
Brigham, Carl, 43
Broca, Paul, 52
Brooklyn, New York, 121
"brown" racism, 109
Brown University, 124
"brute" image, 68
Burgess, John W., 29
Bush, George H. W., 17, 74, 98, 99,
102
Bush, Jeb, 102
California: and affirmative action,
86, 87; Republican, 93. *See also*
Los Angeles; Oakland; San
Francisco
Carr, John, 59
Carr, Peter, 58, 59
Carr, Samuel, 58, 59
Carter, James Earl (Jimmy), 96
Cartwright, Samuel W., 28, 52
caste, 60-63, 77

castration, 30, 32
Catholics, 23, 25, 26
Caucasian (Caucasoid) race
category, 3, 6, 27, 28, 29; and
domination, 46, 108; and
hierarchy, 40, 107, 108, 139;
phenotype, 80; stereotypes, 52, 59
Cayton, Horace, 40
CEEB (College Entrance
Examination Board), 43
census, 7
Central Park Jogger case, 16, 74, 75
Chang, Iris, 123
Chase-Riboud, Barbara, 55, 57
Chase, Allen, 52
Cheney, Richard, 102
Chicago, Illinois, 91
China: racism in, 122, 123; and skin
color bias, 109, 120
"Chinaman", 119
Chinese-Americans, 120; "brown
racism" of, 109; discrimination
against, 120-122. *See also* Lin;
Ma
Christianity and racism, 30, 31. *See
also* Catholics; Protestants
civil rights, 80, 82, 83, 91, 129
Civil Rights Act of 1866, 93
Civil Rights Act of 1964, 84, 85, 87-
88, 104; Title VII of the, 110, 113,
115, 117
class system, 44, 60-63, 128
Cleveland, Ohio, 82
Clinton, Hillary, 103
Clinton, William Jefferson (Bill), 99-
100, 102, 118, 120
Cobett, William, 55
colleges: and affirmative action, 79,
80, 85, 88, 89; and discrimination,
81, 86, 87, 90, 104
colonization and bias, 107-108
color bias. *See* dark skin color;
lawsuits; light skin color; racism

"colorblind society", 129, 130, 131, 132-133
color symbolism. *See* stereotype; symbolism
Committee on Equal Employment Opportunity, 85
Committee on Government Contracts, 84, 85
Congressional Record, 80
Conservative Citizens Council, 104
Costenos, 109
Crain's New York Business, 15
Cuba, 109
culture, American, 47

dark skin color: and employment discrimination, 111, 112-113; Filipino, 109; Puerto Rican, 110-111; and sexuality, 57; stigma, 109; symbolism, 127-128. *See also* racism; skin color; stereotype
Darwin, Charles, 38, 51
Davidson, Rachel, 1124
Davis, L., 77
"Declaration of Independence", 27, 55
Declining Significance of Race, The (Wilson), 40
Democratic Party, 93, 94, 95-96, 99-100
Democratic-Republican Party, 94
denigration, 8; African-American, 34, 53, 68; of biracial offspring, 123; and education, 131-132; and racism, 53; and science, 51.
Devine, P., 76
differentiation, and race, 3
discrimination: Chinese ethnic, 120; color-based, 125; employment, 110, 111; light skin, 114-118; passive, 90; and power, 108; reverse, 80, 81, 86. *See also* lawsuits; skin color discrimination

Diseases and Peculiarities of the Negro (Cartwright), 52-53
divorce, 13
DNA, 58, 59
dominance, 107, 108, 128
dominant group norm, 109
dominant group privilege, 25, 27, 42, 43, 44
Douglas, Sidney, 114
Drew, Charles, 53
DuBois, W.E.B., 39-40, 48
Duke, David, 97, 98

economics: and class, 62; and minority incomes, 110; and quality of life, 10, 99; of slavery, 48
education: and dropouts, 12; and power, 12; racism in, 131-132. *See also colleges by specific name;* CEEB; IQ tests
Edwards, Edwin W., 97
ego, 31, 33
Egyptians, 65-66
Ehrlich, Howard, 68
Eisenhower, Dwight, 82, 84, 85, 96
"Emancipation Proclamation", 27, 34, 93, 103
employment, 80, 82, 83, 84; discrimination, 110, 111
England, 22, 24, 25, 26, 132
environment and race, 41
equal employment opportunities (EEO), 81, 85, 114-115. *See also* affirmative action
Erickson, Steve, 57
"Essay on Population" (Malthus), 52
Ethiopia, 19, 65
eugenics, 79
Euro-American(s): miscegenation, 118; and politics, 140; as racists, 110, 124, 127, 129, 130-131; superiority of, 130, 133-135

Eurocentrism, 134-136, 137, 140
Europe: agricultural economy of, 34;
    colonization by, 107-108
European slaves, 20, 21-22
exclusion, 46, 80, 107
Executive Order 1124, 85

Fair Employment Practices
    Commission, 84
Far Eastern Economic Review, The
    123
Farmer, James, 82
Felero v Stryker, 112-113
Felix v Marquez, 111-112
Filipinos: "brown racism" of, 109;
    mixed marriage in, 123. *See also*
    miscegenation
film and stereotypes, 70-73
Fiske, John, 29
Fite, Virginia, 114
Florida election fraud, 102
Foster, Jobling, Taylor, Donnelly, de
    Knijff, Mieremet, Zerjal, and
    Tyler-Smith, 58, 59
Fourteenth Amendment, 86, 87, 88,
    117
Franklin, John Hope, 120
Frazier, Franklin, 40
"free African-Americans", 55, 60, 61
Freud, Sigmund, 30, 31, 127

genetics, 54, 58-59
Georgia, 114-115
German-Americans, 95
Gingrich, Newt, 100, 102
Gore, Albert, Jr., 99, 102
Gould, Stephen Jay, 52
Graham, H., 83
Greeks, 65-66, 67
Griffe, 60
group privilege, 47, 48. *See also*
    dominant group privilege

Haiti, 25
Hall, Ronald, 55, 80, 115
Hamitic tribes, 30, 31, 32
Hanger, John, 103
Harris, Katherine, 102
Harvard Educational Revue, 69
Harvard Law School, 132
Hatch, Orrin, 81
Hawkins, John, 25
Hemings, Betty, 55
Hemings, Eston, 58, 59
Hemings, Sally, 55-59, 60
Herodotus, 66
Herrnstein, Richard, 70
Herrnstein and Murray, 35, 139
hierarchy, 37, 40, 128; absurdity of,
    108. *See also* racial hierarchy;
    skin color hierarchy
Hispanic-Americans, 14, 118
Hispaniola, 25
Hoetink, Harry, 67
Hoff, 82
Hogue, 122
Hood, 82
Horton, Willie, 17, 74, 98-99, 130
"How Much Can We Boost IQ and
    Scholastic Achievement?"
    (Jensen), 69
Hubbard, R., 52
*Human Behavior in the Social
    Environment* (Zastrow and Kirst-
    Ashman), 137
id, 31, 33
identity: and phenotype, 128; and
    race, 81
Illinois, 91, 115-118
imagery, racist, 67-77
immigration: American, 133; of
    "inferior" races, 42-43; laws, 43;
    policies, 7
income, 110
India, 67, 109
Indonesia, 120

inferiority, 48, 51-52; of Africans,
21, 34-35; of African-Americans.
53; and biology, 88-89; Negroid,
8; of other race groups, 43, 122;
and racism, 109
ingroup, 68
IQ, 67, 77; and race, 42, 69-70; tests,
41, 42, 43, 69-70
Irish-Americans, 95
Italy, 19

Jackson, Jesse, 120
Jamaica, 25
Jamestown, Virginia, 25-26
Japanese racism, 122-123
Jefferson, Eston Hemings, 58, 59
Jefferson, Field, 58, 59
Jefferson, Polly, 56
Jefferson, Thomas, 55-60, 94
Jensen, Arthur, 69, 70
Jews, 43
Johnson, Charles S., 40
Johnson, Lyndon, 82, 83, 85
Johnson, Ralph, 124
Jones, R. L., 91
*Journal of Sociology and Social
Welfare,* 80
judicial bias, 109

Katz and Braly, 73
Kennedy, John F., 82, 83, 85
King, Martin Luther, Jr., 104
King, Rodney, 123
Koreans: racism of, 122, 123; and
skin color bias, 119, 121
Ku Klux Klan, 97

language, 15, 27-28; English, 119;
Spanish, 15; terms of color bias,
74, 84, 118-120, 123, 127-128
Latino-Americans, 5, 7, 47, 86
law enforcement. *See* New Jersey;
New York City; police

laws: bias and the, 109; labor, 80.
See also affirmative action
lawsuits: Bakke, 81, 86, 87-88; color
bias, 109, 110, 111-118; by
people of color, 115, 118
Lewis, Ruby, 114
light skin color, 31; discrimination,
114-118; and lawsuits, 110-111;
and power, 108; in Puerto Rico,
110-113; and racism, 107; and
social position, 62. *See also*
mulatto; "passing"
Lin, Mee Ying, 120
Lincoln, Abraham, 27, 93
Linnaeus, 52
Lippmann, 67
Lombardo, B., 68
Los Angeles, California, 121, 123
"Los Negritos", 10
Lott, Trent, 103-104
Louisiana, 97
lynching, 32, 133

Ma, Ying, 118-122, 123
machismo. *See* masculinity
Malthus, 52
Man Called Hawk, A (tv), 76-77
marriage. *See* mixed-race; power
marry downward, 11
"marry light", 54
marry upward, 11
Marsh, 65
masculinity, 10
Massachusetts, 17, 75-76
"master status", 109
*McDonnell Douglas Corporation v
Green,* 113
McIntosh, P., 89, 133
Meany, George, 84, 85
media stereotypes, 14, 16-18, 70-77
Mestizos, 109
Mexican-Americans, unemployed,
10

minority designation, 37
miscegenation: African-American,
    53-54; defined, 53; Euro-
    American, 118; increasing, 124
Mismeasure of Man (Gould), 52
Mississippi, 25, 103, 104
mixed race, 54, 55; American origins
    of, 61; and class, 62; mulatto, 56,
    60-63. *See also* African-
    Americans; black/white
    dichotomy
Mongoloid race category, 3, 4, 7, 15;
    and racism, 45-46, 47. *See also*
    Asian-Americans; Latino-
    Americans; Native Americans
Morton, Samuel George, 52
mulatto, 56, 60-63; defined, 60;
    "marginal", 62-63
Myrdal, Gunnar, 8, 53

NAACP, 85
National Commission on Working
    Women, 11
Native Americans (Indians), 5, 8, 47;
    employment of, 118; as slaves,
    20, 25, 31
Negroid: beauty, 66; bias and the law
    and, 13; is a composite, 28, 29-30;
    and genetics, 54; as inferior, 8;
    language and, 15; race category,
    3, 4, 7, 33, 44; and racism, 45-46;
    stereotypes, 65-66, 127-128; as
    superior, 51. *See also* African-
    Americans; Latino-Americans
New Deal, 95, 95
New Jersey, 14-15, 73
New York, 103, 121
New York City, 15, 16, 74-75, 120
New York Times, 59, 101
Nguyen, Philip, 121
Nicaragua, 109
Nixon, Richard, 82-83, 84, 85, 100-
    102

"Noble Savage", 51
Nordics, 43
norm, 81; dominant group, 109;
    images, 66-67
North Carolina, 86
Nott, Josiah C., 28

Oakland, California, 118
octoroon, 60
Office of the Commonwealth of
    Puerto Rico (OCCPRW), 111,
    112
Office of Federal Contract
    Compliance (OFCC), 82
Ohio, 82
"one drop" theory, 54
Oregon, 93
outgroup, 68-69

Pakistan, 109
Paris, France, 56
Park, Robert ,40
"passing", for another race, 58
patriarchy, 13
"people of color": defined, 110;
    lawsuits by, 115, 118; and racism,
    107, 108, 109, 118, 136, 137. *See
    also* lawsuits
Perry, Lincoln Theodore Monroe
    Andrew, 71
phenotype, 28, 30; African, 30, 34;
    Caucasian, 80; mulatto, 62; and
    race identification, 128. *See also*
    Jefferson, Thomas
Philadelphia, Pennsylvania, 26, 61,
    82, 85
Philadelphia Plan, 82, 83
Philænion, 66
Philippines. *See* Filipinos
Phillips, Ulrich B., 29
Philodemus, 66
Philostratus, 67
photographs, and bias, 16-17, 75-76

plantation culture, 33, 34
Podhoretz, Norman, 16
police: assaults by, 16; racial bias of, 13, 14, 15, 16
Porter v the State of Illinois, 115-117
Portugal, 19
Powell, Lewis F., Jr., 88
power: and affirmative action, 90-91; and discrimination, 108; dominant group, 41, 42, 108-109; and light skin, 107; and masculinity, 10; and privilege, 25, 27; and quality of life, 91; and racism, 131, 132-133; and slavery, 25; women's, 91
Presstronics, 117-118
Princeton, New Jersey, 73
projection, 32, 33, 127-128
Protestants, 23
Providence, Rhode Island, 124
Puerto Rico: color stereotypes in, 110-111; light skin ideals in, 110-113

quadroon, 60
Quakers, 23-24, 26
quality of life, 8. 10, 11, 18, 91
quotas, 7, 82

race: African-American sensitivity and, 13; and aggression, 4; and American's evolution, 8, 39, 128; biology of, 6, 128-129; categories, 37; complexity of, 6; defined, 3, 4, 44; and evolution, 41, 139; fantasies, 31; genesis of, 37-38; and heredity, 41; and identity, 81; and inferiority, 3-5, 9; and intelligence, 42, 69-70; judicial, 14, 15; as myth, 38-39, 40; rhetoric, 10, 138; and science, 28-29, 41-43, 128-129, 133. *See also*

dominant group privilege; IQ; races; slavery
"Race Initiative" panel, 118, 120
races. *See* Caucasian; Mongoloid; Negroid
race groups. *See* Jews; Nordics; Slavs
racial curiosity, 65
racial divide, 90
racial hierarchy, 27, 28-29, 35, 37, 40, 139; and civil rights, 86; European roots of, 45; post-WWII, 129
racial images, 67-70, 72-77. *See also* stereotype
racial privilege, 40, 41
racial profiling, 15
racism: in advertising, 122; by African-Americans, 79, 124; in American life, 45; and biology, 46, 107, 133; "black", 120-121, 122; and the black/white dichotomy, 107-108, 124; "brown", 109; and Caucasian dominance, 108; and Christianity, 30, 31; cruelty of, 108; and dark skin, 16; defined, 45, 49, 107-108, 124, 130-131; and denigration, 53; in education, 131-132; Euro-American, 48, 107-108; evolving, 134; imagery of, 67-77; institutional, 133; intensity of, 79; Mongoloid race group, 45-46, 47; among Negroids, 45-46; in New Jersey, 14-15; origins, 45, 48; persists, 109; politics of, 48; and power, 108-109, 132-133; and quotas, 7; and science, 52-53, 108; in a sociological context, 45, 46, 107, 109; as a tool of oppression, 45; 21st century, 109, 118, 120; victims of, 47; "white", 109. *See also* Atlantic slave trade;

Euro-Americans; language; lawsuits; Ma; media stereotypes; police; stereotype; "white supremacy"
radio and stereotypes, 73
Randolph, Elmo, 14
Randolph, Martha Jefferson, 58
rape fantasy, 72
Rape of Nanking, The (Chang), 123
Reagan, Ronald, 81, 98
Red Cross, 53
"red-haired devils", 123
Republican Party: and abolition, 93, 94; African-Americans in the, 94, 96; early, 94-95; modern, 97-99, 100-105; origins, 93; racism of the, 93, 97, 98, 100, 102, 103-105; and slavery, 93. *See also* Bush; Eisenhower; Lincoln; Nixon; Reagan
"reverse discrimination", 80, 81, 86
Rhode Island, 124
Rodney, Walter, 52
Roosevelt, Franklin, 96
Rousseau, J., 51
Russell, Wilson, and Hall, 55

"Sambo" image, 68
San Francisco, California, 121
science: and denigration, 51; and genetics, 54, 58-59; and inferiority, 87-89; and race, 28-29, 41-43, 128-129, 133; and racism, 52-53, 108
Scottsboro Boys case, 18
segregation, 5, 33
Settlement House, 91
sexuality, 57, 60, 72, 119
Sharpton, Al, 120
Skelton, Martha Wayles, 55-56
skin color: and exclusion, 80; publications about, 137; and racism, 107, 108. *See also* China;

dark skin color; Filipino; Japan; Korea; light skin color; masculinity
skin color discrimination, 110-125
skin color hierarchy, 122-123
slavery: abolitionists and, 23, 28; criticized, 23-24; economics of, 48, 52; end of, 24, 26, 27; and labor needs, 52; legacy of, 4, 8, 18; power and, 25; sexualized, 32; and trade goods, 23. *See also* Atlantic slave trade; slaves
slaves: African, 19-28, 29; Caucasian, 35; European, 20, 21-22; Islamic, 20; Native American, 20, 25, 31; South American, 25, 26; women as, 22, 60. *See also* Atlantic slave trade; slavery
Slavs, 43
Smith, Al, 95
Smith, Dinitia, 59
Smith, Susan, 75-76
social science, 128
social structures, 44
Social Works Abstracts, 137
social work textbooks, 137
"somatic norm image", 67
Sotomayor, M., 10
South America, 24, 26
South Carolina, 33
Southeast Asian Community Center, 121
Spain, 19
Specter, Arlen, 103, 104
Spenser for Hire (TV), 77
Sri Lanka, 109
status quo, 49
Stember, C., 57
Stepin Fetchit, 70-73
stereotype: of African-American men, 67-77; African slave, 33-34; of beauty, 65-67; Caucasoid, 52; Chinese, 119; exploitation, 130; in

films, 70-73; genetics of physicality of the African-American male, 19-20, 24-25, 27, 29; "inferior", 51, 52; in media, 14, 16-18, 98; Negroid inferior, 34-35, 52, 69, 127; political, 98; Puerto Rican, 110-111; racist, 13-18, 109; radio, 73; sexual, 119; television, 74-77
St. Louis, Missouri, 82
Stuart murder case, 75-76
super-ego, 31
symbolism: of black color, 30, 31, 32, 127; of "dirt", 127-128; Oedipal, 32

television, and black stereotypes, 17, 74-74, 76-77, 98
Texas, 86
Theocritus, 66
Third World, 7
Thomas, H., 19
Thurman, Strom, 103
TIME magazine, 17, 76
Title VII, 110, 113, 115, 117
Truman, Harry, 96

unemployment: African-American, 9-10, 11-13; and parenting, 10; psychological impact of, 10; and quality of life, 10; and women, 9
unions, 80, 82, 83-85
United States Bureau of Census, 7
United States Department of Justice, 15, 101
United States Department of Labor, 9, 82
United States Supreme Court, 87-88
University of California, 87
University of Michigan, 90
University of North Carolina, 86

Vietnamese, 119

Virginia, 25-26
Voting Rights Act, 93, 104

Wade, Nicholas, 59
Walker v the Internal Revenue Service (IRS), 114-115
Walker, Tracy, 114
Washington, Booker T., 39
Washington, R., 109
Watergate scandal, 100-101
Wayles, John, 55
Whig Party, 93, 94
"white", 67, 111-112, 118, 120
"white man's burden", 31
"white privilege", 89-90, 133. *See also* racism
"white" racism, 109
"white supremacy", 4, 39, 40, 51, 54, 73, 104-105; and affirmative action, 79, 129, 130
Williams, Marcia, 116
Williams, Vanessa, 57
Wilson, William Julius, 40
Woodson, Thomas, 58, 59
women: empowered, 91; Euro-American field working, 25; as slaves, 22, 60. *See also* African-American women; slaves

X, Malcolm, 158

Zastrow and Kirst-Ashman, 137

SYMPOSIUM SERIES

1.   Jïrgen Moltmann *et al.*, **Religion and Political Society**
2.   James Grace, **God, Sex, and the Social Project: Glassboro Papers on Religion and Human Sexuality**
3.   M. Darroll Bryant and Herbert W. Richardson (eds.), **A Time for Consideration: A Scholarly Appraisal of the Unification Church**
4.   Donald G. Jones, **Private and Public Ethics: Tensions Between Conscience and Institutional Responsibility**
5.   Herbert W. Richardson, **New Religions and Mental Health: Understanding the Issues**
6.   Sheila Greeve Davaney (ed.), **Feminism and Process Thought: The Harvard Divinity School / Claremont Center for Process Studies Symposium Papers**
7.   A.T.D./Fourth World, **Children of Our Time: Words and Lives of Fourth World Children**
8.   Jenny Yates Hammett, **Woman's Transformations: A Psychological Theology**
9.   S. Daniel Breslauer, **A New Jewish Ethics**
10. Darrell J. Fasching (ed.), **Jewish People in Christian Preaching**
11. Henry Vander Goot, **Interpreting the Bible in Theology and the Church**
12. Everett Ferguson, **Demonology of the Early Christian World**
13. Marcia Sachs Littell, **Holocaust Education: A Resource Book for Teachers and Professional Leaders**
14. Char Miller, **Missions and Missionaries in the Pacific**
15. John S. Peale, **Biblical History as the Quest for Maturity**
16. Joseph Buijs, **Christian Marriage Today: Growth or Breakdown**
17. Michael Oppenheim, **What Does Revelation Mean for the Modern Jew?**
18. Carl F.H. Henry, **Conversations with Carl Henry: Christianity for Today**
19. John Biermans, **The Odyssey of New Religious Movements: Persecution, Struggle, Legitimation. A Case Study of the Unification Church**
20. Eugene Kaellis and Rhoda Kaellis (eds.), **Toward a Jewish America**
21. Andrew Wilson (ed.), **How Can the Religions of the World be Unified?: Interdisciplinary Essays in Honor of David S.C. Kim**
22. Marcia Sachs Littell *et al.*, (eds.), **The Holocaust Forty Years After**
23. Ian H. Angus, **George Grant's Platonic Rejoinder to Heidegger: Contemporary Political Philosophy and the Question of Technology**
24. George E. Clarkson, **Grounds for Belief in Life After Death**
25. Herbert W. Richardson, **On the Problem of Surrogate Parenthood: Analyzing the Baby M Case**
26. Leslie Muray, **An Introduction to the Process-Understanding of Science, Society, and the Self: A Philosophy for Modern Man**
27. Dan Cohn-Sherbok (ed.), **The Salman Rushdie Controversy**
28. James Y. Holloway (ed.), **Barth, Barmen and the Confessing Church: *Katallegate***
29. Ronald F. Duska (ed.), ***Rerum Novarum*–A Symposium Celebrating 100 Years of Catholic Social Thought**
30. Franklin H. Littell, Alan L. Berger, and Hubert G. Locke (eds.), **What Have We Learned?: Telling the Story and Teaching the Lessons of the Holocaust: Papers of the 20th Annual Scholars' Conference**
31. Alan L. Berger (ed.), **Bearing Witness to the Holocaust, 1939-1989**

32. G. Jan Colijn and Marcia S. Littell (eds.), **The Netherlands and Nazi Genocide: Papers of the 21st Annual Scholars' Conference**

33. Marion Mushkat, **Philo-Semitic and Anti-Jewish Attitudes in Post-Holocaust Poland**

34. Katharine B. Free (ed.), **The Formulation of Christianity by Conflict Through the Ages**

35. W. Anthony Gengarelly, **Distinguished Dissenters and Opposition to the 1919-1920 Red Scare**

36. John J. Carey (ed.), **The Sexuality Debate in North American Churches 1988-1995: Controversies, Unresolved Issues, Future Prospects**

37. James P. Hurd (ed.), **Investigating the Biological Foundations of Human Morality**

38. Allen E. Hye, **The Moral Dilemma of the Scientist in Modern Drama: The Inmost Force**

39. Will Morrisey, **A Political Approach to Pacifism (2 Volumes - 39A-39B)**

40. LaRae Larkin, **The Legitimacy in International Law of the Detention and Internment of Aliens and Minorities in the Interest of National Security**

41. Brian L. Fife, **School Desegregation in the Twenty-First Century: The Focus Must Change**

42. Paul Leslie (ed.), **The Gulf War as Popular Entertainment: An Analysis of the Military-Industrial Media Complex**

43. Jutta T. Bendremer, **Women Surviving the Holocaust: In Spite of the Horror**

44. George Anastaplo, **Campus Hate-Speech Codes, Natural Right, and Twentieth Century Atrocities**

45. David Brez Carlisle, **Human Sex Change and Sex Reversal: Transvestism and Transsexualism**

46. Jack Parsons, **Human Population Competition: A Study of the Pursuit of Power Through Numbers (2 Volumes - 46A-46B)**

47. Adam Neuman-Nowicki, **Struggle for Life During the Nazi Occupation of Poland**, translated and edited by Sharon Stambovsky Strosberg

48. Christopher G. Hudson, **An Interdependency Model of Homelessness: The Dynamics of Social Disintegration**

49. Michèle Chaban, **The Life Work of Dr. Elisabeth Kübler-Ross and Its Impact on the Death Awareness Movement**

50. Englebert Ssekasozi, **A Philosophical Defense of Affirmative Action**

51. Kimmo Kääriäinen, **Religion in Russia After the Collapse of Communism: Religious Renaissance or Secular State**

52. Edward Timms and Andrea Hammel (eds.), **The German-Jewish Dilemma: From the Enlightenment to the Shoah**

53. Victoria La' Porte, **An Attempt to Understand the Muslim Reaction to the Satanic Verses**

54. Elizabeth S. Spragins, **Metaphoric Analysis of the Debate on Physician Assisted Suicide**

55. Alice Duhon-Ross (ed.), **Reaching and Teaching Children Who Are Victims of Poverty**

55. Alice Duhon-Ross (ed.), **Reaching and Teaching Children Who Are Victims of Poverty**

56. Joan C. McClennen and John Gunther (eds.), **A Professional's Guide to Understanding Gay and Lesbian Domestic Violence: Understanding Practice Interventions**

57. Seamus Dunn and Helen Dawson, **An Alphabetical Listing of Word, Name and Place in Northern Ireland and the Living Language of Conflict**

58. Alexandre Kimenyi and Otis L. Scott (eds.), **Anatomy of Genocide: State-Sponsored Mass-Killings in the Twentieth Century**

59. Margaret Phipps Brown, Samuel L. Dameron, Richard H. Moore, **The Role of Firearms in Domestic Violence: A Study of Victims, Police, and Domestic Violence Shelter Workers in West Virginia**

60. Patricia Ainsa, **Teaching Children With AIDS**

61. J. Sanford Rikoon and Theresa L. Goedeke, **Anti-Environmentalism and Citizen Opposition to the Ozark Man and the Biosphere Reserve**

62. Jules Steinberg, **Hannah Arendt on the Holocaust: A Study of the Suppression of Truth**

63. Stephen Gilliatt, **An Exploration of the Dynamics of Collaboration and Non-Resistance**

64. Lola M. Butler, Diane Elliott, John Gunther (eds.), **Strategies to Overcome Oppression and Discrimination for Marginalized Groups**

65. Douglas B. Reynolds, **Scarcity and Growth Considering Oil and Energy: An Alternative Neo-Classical View**

66. Steven L. Spiegel, Jennifer D. Kibbe, Elizabeth G. Matthews (eds.), **The Dynamics of Middle East Nuclear Proliferation**

67. Darlington I. I. Ndubuike, **The Struggles, Challenges and Triumphs of the African Immigrants in America**

68. Kathleen M. Sweet, **Terrorism and Airport Security**

69. Michael P. Tkacik, **The Future of U.S. Nuclear Operational Doctrine: Balancing Safety and Deterrence in an Anarchic World**

70. Ronald E. Hall, **Discrimination Among Oppressed Populations**

71. Gwendolyn C. Shealy, **A Critical History of the American Red Cross, 1882-1945: The End of Noble Humanitarianism**

72. Ronald E. Hall, **Skin Color as a Post-Colonial Issue Among Asian-Americans**

73. To be announced

74. Jacques J. Rozenberg (ed.), **Bioethical and Ethical Issues Surrounding the Trials and Code of Nuremberg: Nuremberg Revisited**

75. Howard Lee Nostrand, **From the Polarizing Mind-Set to Productive Discussion of Public Policy and Intercultural and Interfaith Relations: Finding Common Ground**

76. Suzanne Ost, **An Analytical Study of the Legal, Moral, and Ethical Aspects of the Living Phenomenon of Euthanasia**

77. Minoru Kiyota (ed.), **The Case of Japanese Americans During World War II: Suppression of Civil Liberty**, assisted by Ronald S. Green

78. Simon P. Sibelman (ed.), **Teaching the Shoah in the Twenty-First Century–Topics and Topographies**

79. Ronald E. Hall, **The Scientific Fallacy and Political Misuse of the Concept of Race**